Rethinking Utility Customer Care

SATISFYING YOUR ALWAYS-CONNECTED, ALWAYS-ON CUSTOMERS

Rethinking Utility Customer Care

SATISFYING YOUR ALWAYS-CONNECTED, ALWAYS-ON CUSTOMERS

Todd W. Arnold

CS Week

Sherman, Texas

To my girls and the boy—they make life beautiful. And to my wonderful parents, who as great schoolteachers, would be shocked I could put this many words on paper.

Table of Contents

Foreword

Any business providing customer service is experiencing a rapid, transformative change to a new digital world. Utilities are no different. Increasingly our customers are choosing to do business with us via digital channels. Additionally, customers are demanding more information and transparency about their energy usage. To provide excellent customer service in this digital age, utilities need to rethink utility customer care. To meet the demands of the always-connected, always-on customers, utilities must anticipate customers' needs, customize their service offerings to each unique customer and serve their customers in their channel of choice, which is increasingly the digital channel.

During my now over 25 years in the utility business, I have watched and managed the transition from predominately offering face-to-face customer service in local business offices, to telephony-based service provided by 24/7 call centers with interactive voice response systems (IVRs), to web-based service. In fact, during my current tenure at Eversource Energy, I have witnessed customer web transactions growing from a mere two percent of transactions in the early 2000's to 58 percent of transactions in 2014. This represents over 13 million customer transactions annually, outstripping any other channels we offer including inbound call center and interactive voice response.

As utilities discuss, plan and transform to the "utility of the future," satisfying the always-connected, always-on customer has to be a fundamental requirement. The implications of meeting these requirements imply investment in the utility distribution infrastructure, in the information technology systems and in the expertise to manage and leverage these tools.

Fortunately, Todd Arnold has provided us with a primer on how to rethink utility customer care and ensure we are satisfying our always-connected and always-on customers. This thought-provoking book offers readers insight into the rapidly changing digital world in which we are living today. Todd explores and explains the implications of this world to the utility—and specifically to utility customer service processes—systems and workforce. Finally, Todd also provides concrete ideas and recommendations that savvy utilities leaders will want to implement to ensure they are well positioned to serve their customers now and into the future.

Todd is a recognized thought leader in utility service with more than 40 years in the business. He served as the senior vice president of smart grid and customer systems at Duke Energy as well as the senior vice president for customer service. Todd's passion has been to enhance utility customers' experiences not only at Duke Energy but throughout the utility industry. As such, he is actively involved in the industry as a speaker and with numerous organizations focused on the customer.

One such organization is CSWeek, where Todd serves on the Board of Directors and chairs the Executive Summit. CS Week has a mission of providing high-quality educational content for water, gas and electric utility customer service experts around the country. In upholding this mission, CS Week offers a not-to-be-missed conference in the spring which features content on the latest utility customer service products, services and processes. I am excited to see CS Week expanding on their mission by now moving into publishing. Todd's *Rethinking Utility Customer Care* will be the first of many customer service publications offered by CSWeek.

Todd's perspective on the changes required for our connected world is important as it is grounded in actual experience. Todd has successfully led large organizations through two merger integrations and has implemented significant transformations to utility customer service models. Todd's implementation of smart grid technologies at Duke Energy was groundbreaking, where he led the $1 billion smart grid initiative to modernize the company's power delivery system and customer interfaces.

I consider *Rethinking Utility Customer Care* a must read. There are so many take-aways I have personally gained from this book. I am thankful to Todd for providing me, my team and customer service leaders across the country with this valuable primer on successfully serving the always-connected, always-on customer. I'm confident readers will gain insights that will cause them to rethink their utility customer care processes and technologies, enabling them to serve their customers uniquely, proactively and in the channel of their choice, thereby creating a superb customer experience.

Penni McLean-Conner
Senior vice president and chief customer officer for Eversource Energy
Author of *Customer Service: Utility Style* and *Energy Efficiency: Principles and Practices*

Acknowledgements

Numerous people gave me time, expertise, insight, and feedback. I can't thank them enough for always responding when I asked for their thoughts: Sue Arnold, Brad Cleveland, Jeff Conklin, Charles Dickerson, Jerry Duvall, Larry Eiser, Frank Hoogendoorn, Rod Litke, Mike Lowe, Penni McLean-Conner, David Merkoski, Dana Moses, Janet Mushrush, Sue O'Leary, Randy Randolph, David Steele, Jamie Wimberly, Mark Wyatt. I also thank Marla Markman for her thoughtful, thorough, patient, persistent and professional editing of this book.

CS Week, a nonprofit educational conference company, provides utility professionals unparalleled access to the leading thinking in all things customer service. I can't thank them enough for their support in publishing my book. It is the first of numerous authors' works they will bring to the utility industry.

In my career, three people took tremendous risks on me, gave me opportunities, provided mentoring, and enabled me to discover my love of utility customer service. They are men of great wisdom and integrity. If not for Larry Thomas, Chuck Winger, and John Procario, I would not have been able to have the experiences required to write this book. Nor would I have had a career beyond anything I imagined.

Finally, and oddly, I must thank Starbucks. When it comes to Starbucks, I just don't get it. At Starbucks, it seems I always wait in line to pay a premium price for coffee that is basically a commodity. Yet I found it to be where I spent most of my time writing this book because it was where I did my best thinking. So, I guess, that is the illogical magic of Starbucks. Millions find something there that works for them beyond the commodity of coffee. Which is a great lesson for us who are schooled in commodity and need to rethink our business for this digitally connected, consumer-empowered world.

Preface

In 2010, after 34 years, I retired from PSI Energy/Cinergy/ Duke Energy, where I spent much of my time in and around utility customer care. I found I could not just walk away from my passion for all things customer service. Fortunately for me, I am fascinated by how digital technologies have transformed the consumer and find myself constantly thinking about their impact on customer care.

In this decade, we have seen a confluence of technologies create a ubiquitous, connected consumer. Everything around us is embedded with digital technology and interfacing with all sorts of things. The result is a consumer who is always connected, always on. This ubiquitous connectivity impacts every aspect of how the consumer lives, works, and plays. Consumers have the world at their fingertips—and they can access it from anyplace, at any time, to immediately solve their problems. This is changing consumers' expectations of customer service and significantly raising the bar for customer experience excellence.

In a way, this consumer technology transformation is happening unnoticed. Consumers have adopted smartphones and their plethora of apps so rapidly and painlessly that these unbelievable new ways of living go generally unnoticed. It appears consumers will continue to easily adopt and absorb the next wave of connected consumer technology: watches, wearables, cars, and homes. I have to believe that when the automobile, electric light, and running water were introduced that people marveled for some time about their life-changing properties. Our adoption of digital technology seems to immediately go mainstream, with us taking it for granted and living as if it has been around for decades.

It is this stealth assimilation into how people live, work, and play that makes it easy for customer service leaders to miss the impact and consequence on what it means for customer care. This book will shine a light on our new digital consumers and connect the dots to build a case for rethinking utility customer care for our connected world.

You will find the book electric utility-centered. I did not mean to exclude gas, water, and wastewater utilities. I simply know electric utilities best. Electric utilities are also where you have a greater digital transformation occurring throughout the utility system and, therefore, a greater ability to deliver the new solutions required by your always-connected, always-on consumers. Even though I don't have examples specific to all utilities, the changes in the consumer and their impact on customer care apply across the board.

The book is not intended to present an exact view of the future. It is to provide a series of observations to provoke thinking on how consumers' massive adoption of digitally connected technologies impacts how you think about your customer care. It is not to be a futurist's view. I consider myself a "nowist" and present issues impacting you today.

Introduction

I had the privilege of working for PSI Energy/Cinergy/Duke Energy for 34 years. Over 20 years of these were under the visionary leadership of chairman and CEO Jim Rogers. In 2007, I was Duke Energy's senior vice president of customer service and found myself in the midst of Jim's vision to build a smarter grid. Jim's chief technology officer, David Mohler, was spearheading the development of Duke Energy's smart grid strategy. I pestered David to tutor me on all things smart grid, and he immersed me in numerous books, white papers, and vendor briefings. I became hooked on the possibilities of smart grid, and in 2008 found myself Duke Energy's SVP of smart grid and customer systems, responsible for building the organization to deploy smart grid at scale.

Throughout this time, up until I retired in 2010, I had a hard time finding the customer in all of the utility industry's "smart" smart grid thinking. As I went through these mounds of material, I was reminded of the "Where's Waldo" children's books, as I found myself repeatedly asking, "Where's the customer?" They would talk about demand response, smart appliances, home energy management systems, smart thermostats, and offerings that would interface with the customer. But it was more of how we would install technology with an unwritten assumption that the customer would embrace it. Numerous smart grid think tanks would draw complex diagrams of smart grid, and if there were customers, they were depicted as a house on the edge of the diagram. I couldn't find a customer-centric view.

Then in 2010, the customer appeared, in a not so positive way, as they raised their social media-empowered voices. A loud and socially powerful minority of customers began to voice their opposition to smart meters based on a variety of issues: privacy, health, safety, and costs. And this began the realization that for smart grid to be successful, the utility industry had to engage customers.

This consumer pushback wasn't because utilities were doing smart grid wrong. In fact, they were doing what they always did: strategizing, designing, and implementing how to modernize the grid so that they continued to deliver affordable, reliable, convenient, and clean energy. This was just more of what utilities have done exceptionally well for over a century.

But this time it was different. Smart energy requires us to go beyond the meter: to provide customers numerous options, to connect to their appliances and home energy management systems, and to change customer behaviors so they reduce how much energy they consume and reduce the demands they put on the grid.

Grid modernization means you have to engage the customer—and this changes the ballgame. As a result, utilities are now challenged to lead the biggest customer experience transformation since they introduced electric living in the '50s and '60s. Today, utilities must build new smart energy competencies around customer segmentation, education, engagement, home energy management systems, dynamic pricing, energy information, gamification, prepay, and more.

But a funny thing has happened on the way to building a smarter grid. The customers got smart first, and they continue to get smarter at a faster rate than the utilities. In the few years utilities have been deploying smart grids, their customers have adopted digital technologies that have resulted in them being always connected, always on. As a result, they literally have the knowledge of the world at their fingertips. The customer is accelerating, at a breathtaking pace, the adoption of smart technologies that are transforming every facet of how they live, work, and play.

HOW THIS BOOK IS ORGANIZED

It is this transformation in the consumer that is driving a need for utilities to rethink customer care, and thus, the central theme of this book. My case is presented sequentially as follows.

In Part I, "Impact," I discuss how ubiquitous digital communication is impacting the utility and the consumer, and its implications.

Regardless of the extent and the speed at which utilities modernize their grid, customers are dramatically modernizing their lives. In Chapter 1, "The Customer Is Smarter Than You," I detail the rate of adoption of digital technologies and how the consumer has advanced beyond the utility. Then in Chapter 2, "And Getting Smarter Faster Than You," I cover how the proliferation of consumer technologies will only accelerate and grow consumer expectations. In Chapter 3, "How Smart Will You Be?," I contrast the speed of change with the consumer and the utility. Then I speak to how it is driving the need to rethink utility customer care for our connected world.

Digital devices and ubiquitous connectivity means the customer is always connected. That means companies have a wealth of new opportunities to interact and converse with their customers. Not in the traditional mass marketing or broadcasting sense but to each customer's specific preferences and needs. This is transforming customers' expectations because they can access anything, at any time, to solve any problem or fulfill any need. This is creating a very different consumer. In Chapter 4, I cover "The New Consumer: Me, Myself & I" and their new requirements.

One of the challenges for smart energy is how to engage a customer that appears to be apathetic in regards to energy. Utilities have done a great job of reliably delivering a mostly invisible product that is not directly consumed and is back-of-mind for the majority of customers. In Chapter 5, "From Back-of-Mind to Engagement and Relationship," I will discuss the need for utilities to engage consumers and build relationships.

This proliferation of consumer technologies is dramatically changing customers' requirements for an excellent customer experience and, therefore, changing the products, programs, and services that they expect. In Part II, "Rethink," I detail how utilities must rethink customer care for our connected world.

The need for a long-term bond or relationship brings with it a new set of customer service requirements. It's one thing to enroll or acquire a customer for a one-time interaction. It's another thing if you want that customer to continue to interact and engage with you and sustain that behavior. In Chapter 6, "Relationship Prerequisites," I lay out the new fundamentals that must permeate all aspects of your customer care if you expect to have any level of sustained engagement with your customers.

In Chapter 7, "Working for Me," I provide a customer-centric view of reliability and why you won't get any points for just improving it. The customer doesn't think in terms of reliability. Like air, we only think of reliability when it doesn't exist. Focusing on reliability improvement is not enough. It is critical that your customers understand how hard you are working for them.

Utilities have done an outstanding job of improving their outage restoration and communication processes. However, customer expectations have outpaced utilities' progress. In Chapter 8, "My Restoration," I discuss that unless you are building the ability to communicate accurately and timely each specific customer's outage and their estimated time of restoration, then you will not be doing enough in customers' and politicians' eyes.

Historically, a key aspect of utility customer service has been the meter-to-cash functions: billing, payment, credit and collections, service on/off/transfer. In a commodity-focused organization, it is key to efficiently and effectively operate these processes. However, in a connected world, where customers have higher expectations and utilities need to engage their customers, meter-to-cash is too narrow of a focus and is an internally focused view rather than a customer-centric one. In Chapter 9, "Meter-to-Me," I update the meter-to-cash functions to reflect the requirements of your connected customers.

The natural urge is to respond to the digital customer by rushing to add new customer service channels, such as mobile, social, and text. Even though you will need to deliver these new channels enabled by personal connectivity, the connected world also has major implications for your existing self-service offerings. All service channels will need to meet a new set of customer expectations. In Chapter 10, "MySelf Service," I explain why self-service is becoming outdated and will not meet your customers' expectations. You must rethink your self-service and deliver "myself service."

The exponential adoption of mobile devices and their apps presents a new channel with a very different set of customer interaction requirements. In Chapter 11, "Fingertip Resolution," I discuss the opportunities, and ensuing customer requirements, for solutions and services delivered through a mobile application. It is not about delivering applications on mobile. It is about providing easy, instantaneous solutions at customers' fingertips.

Smart digital devices create a level of intimacy because they are always by our side and a level of immediacy because they can solve our problem now. This means we no longer have to broadcast a one-size-fits-all marketing message to the masses. Because these digital devices provide a connection to individual customers, communication and services can now effectively and affordably be tailored to specific consumers. In Chapter 12, "In the Key of Me," we will discuss what I believe to be the significant opportunity for utilities to build a sustained relationship with their customers: the ability to have conversations that are tailored to each customer, with the information that is important and impactful to each of them.

All this change in how customers interact with your company has the potential to reduce the call volume handled by customer service representatives (CSRs). However, the bigger impact is on how it will make the role your CSRs play even more important. As more and more simple and standard interactions are handled by self-service, the calls your CSRs must handle will become even more complex. And they will be coming from customers whose connectivity has enabled them to be as smart as your representatives. In Chapter 13,

"The New CSR: Customer Service Resolutionary," I will discuss the changes required in your call center.

How should customer service leaders respond to this transformation? In Part III, "Go," I discuss strategies for how to approach the customer service transformation. The key to remember is that transformations are always journeys. They are marathons, not sprints. The key is to act, to move, and to implement. It is impossible to get there quickly and in one fell swoop. In Chapter 14, "Think Big, Smart Starts," I will lay out a road map for a successful journey.

Many of these new services demanded by the Me, Myself & I consumer will be through electronic channels. Mostly because this is how the consumer wants them delivered. As the number of customer interaction channels proliferates, it is natural to chase the latest technology. I remember in the late '90s when corporate communications departments began to set up corporate websites and installed a "contact us" button because it was what everyone was doing—only to find some months later the mailbox was full of customer service-related emails no one was answering. Today, many companies have embraced Twitter and Facebook without a clear understanding of the corresponding customer service strategy. Whether you wanted it or not, once you have opened a social media channel, you have created a de facto customer contact channel. In Chapter 15, "Customer Access Strategy," I will show why it is critical for your organization to define each channel, the services to offer, the customers to offer them to, the level of accessibility, and the quality of service.

Often major change initiatives focus on the process and technology changes required while underestimating the importance of the people aspects of the transformation. In Chapter 16, "Customer Care Culture Assessment," I will highlight the steps necessary to identify the changes and initiatives required in your culture if you wish to be successful in this transformation.

As the utility industry has begun to understand the importance of engaging the customer with smart energy, it is my belief the industry is still missing a key ingredient of the smart energy taxonomy. And that is the transformation required of the customer service infrastructure to deliver these services at scale. As stated previously, utility services have historically involved reading the meter, billing the meter, collecting the payment, turning-on/off/transferring service and outage reporting, primarily supported with a legacy customer information system, call center, and website. This system is evolving into a multichanneled, integrated communication, conversational, segmented, dynamic customer experience. In Chapter 17, "A New Customer Service Framework," I will discuss the required transformation of the customer service platform.

It is easy for authors to paint Pollyanna pictures of what should be done. The reality is that each company is unique, with its own set of contexts within which a leader must operate. Chapter 18, "Universal Smart Starts," presents a series of opportunities that should work within any context.

Electric utilities being the last large regulated monopoly model standing make it different from any other industry. Much of that difference makes the rewards and punishments very different. That makes how things happen in this industry, and the pace at which they happen, very different. It presents major obstacles we must overcome if we are to meet our customers' expectations in their digital world. In Chapter 19, "Go Crazy!," I will present a number of thoughts regarding the industry's unique characteristics, how they impact our ability to do the right thing for our customers, and the new models that need to be developed to become a customer-centric industry.

These are exciting times for utility customer care leaders. Ubiquitous digital connectivity provides limitless opportunities to engage and wow our customers. It is time to rethink customer care for our digital world.

PART I

Impact

CHAPTER 1

The Customer Is Smarter Than You

THE BEGINNING

The average consumer would be surprised to know, from a monitoring and control standpoint, that utilities have been isolated from the distribution system: the meter and the customer. Historically, utilities have not been able to cost-justify the connection of communication networks and control equipment to their entire system. It has only made economic sense to connect to the most critical sections of their major transmission networks.

As a result, the majority of utilities depend on the customer to call and notify them when utility equipment malfunctions and causes an outage. The utility must then dispatch a truck to find the specific location of the outage, investigate the cause, and fix the problem.

Recently, a convergence of factors is driving the need for utilities to replace their century-old isolated analog system with a digitally connected intelligent network. For electric utilities, increased environmental restrictions on generation, the intermittent nature of renewable generation such as wind and solar, growing transmission constraints, and the potential for significant electric vehicle load distributed throughout the system is creating the need for more effective ways to manage load and reduce peak demands. Another factor is the introduction of small distributed generation sources, like solar, into a grid designed primarily for large centralized generation. Plus, today's digital economy demands more reliable power, better outage communication, and faster restoration. For water and gas utilities, the drive is more evolutionary than revolutionary. Because of the lack of a local power source, longer payback periods, and little regulatory push, the digitalization of the water and gas utility will take longer. Yet there are specific applications where gas and water utilities find it beneficial to connect to their grid, their meters, and their customers to improve operations, usage analysis, conservation, and leak detection.

Fortunately, as these factors have developed, digital communication and connectivity have become omnipresent, faster, and more affordable. Thus, it has enabled the two transformations that are requiring utilities to rethink customer care.

1. *The Smart Grid:* As these technologies became more affordable, electric utilities began evaluating and planning for a more intelligent grid. These efforts were jump-started by significant federal legislation. In December 2007, Title XIII of the Energy Independence and Security Act was passed providing federal policy support for a smarter grid.[1] In 2009, as part of the American Recovery and Reinvestment Act, the Department of Energy announced funding of $3.3 billion for the Smart Grid Investment Grants Program and $615 million for smart grid demonstration projects.[2]

2. *The Smart Consumer:* What had begun years earlier as a cellular phone system for mobile voice communica-

tion, "can you hear me now?" expanded into a ubiquitous data network with significant mobile computing capabilities. The release of the first iPhone on June 29, 2007,[3] the opening of the Apple App Store on July 10, 2008,[4] and the release of the first commercially available Android smartphone on October 22, 2008, began the transformation of consumers' cellphones into mobile computing devices.

FAST FORWARD TO TODAY

U.S. utilities have installed over 45 million smart electric meters. This includes thirteen large utilities that are essentially complete with close to 19 million smart meters installed. Another six large utilities are at least 85 percent complete with over 17 million smart meters installed.[5] These utilities that have reached a degree of scale in their deployment are beginning to offer more information on energy usage, and some are beginning to offer new time-based pricing programs.

While utilities have been busy working on a smarter grid, an interesting thing happened with their customers: They got smart first.

According to Pew Internet research, of the 90 percent of American adults who are cell phone owners, the majority (58 percent) own a smartphone of some kind. Additionally, the growth of connectivity through the tablet has been phenomenal, with 42 percent of adults now owning a tablet computer.[6]

Consumers worldwide have connected to over 800 million devices running the iOS platform (iPod Touch, iPhone, iPad).[7] They've established over 800 million Apple iTunes accounts where they can choose from over 1.2 million apps and have done so over 75 billion times. Over 300 million people visit Apple's App Store every week.[8] Additionally, consumers worldwide connected with over 900 million devices running on the Android platform.[9] With over 1.3 million applications available to choose from,[10] consumers are downloading Android applications at the rate of 1 billion a month.[11] And to think, just a few years earlier for both the utility and the consumer, all these millions and billions were basically *zero*!

Throughout this book, I often use the term "smart." Dictionary.com defines "smart" as "having or showing quick intelligence or ready mental capability."[12] I acknowledge "smart" may be an overused term. But it clearly fits the impact that ubiquitous mobile digital connectivity has had on consumers. They now have "quick intelligence and ready mental capability" because of what they have at their connected fingertips.

The truth is, your customers are now smarter than you. While utilities were deploying tens of millions of meters, the consumer was buying hundreds of millions of devices and interacting billions of times.

It bears repeating: A funny thing happened on the way to a smarter grid—customers got smart first. Thanks to their trusty "sidekick," they are now always connected, always on, more digital, more social, more informed, and always up to date. And why not? They have the world at their fingertips.

CHAPTER 2

And Getting Smarter Faster Than You

YOU AIN'T SEEN NOTHING YET

According to Cisco, in 2013, global mobile data traffic grew 81 percent, reaching 1.5 exabytes per month, up from 820 petabytes a year earlier. Mobile data traffic in 2013 was 18 times the size of the entire global Internet in 2000. Of the mobile traffic in 2013, video represented the majority at 53 percent. In 2013, 526 million mobile devices and connections were added. Smartphones made up 77 percent of that growth, with 406 million net additions. Mobile network speeds more than doubled to 1,387 Kbps, up from 526 Kbps a year earlier. As did the average smartphone usage of 529 MB per month versus 353 MB in 2012.

Looking forward, Cisco projects:

- Monthly global mobile data traffic will surpass 15 exabytes by 2018.
- Smartphones will comprise over 66 percent of mobile data traffic by 2018.
- 4G traffic will make up more than half of the total mobile traffic by 2018.

- Tablets will exceed 15 percent of global mobile data traffic by 2016.[13]

CUSTOMERS ARE GETTING SMARTER FASTER THAN YOU

These technology milestones mean the consumer now has the ability to access limitless resources on the Internet at any point, day or night. Dick Tracy watches and Star Trek communicators are no longer fantastical toys—they are now an affordable reality with smartphones, tablets, and smart watches.

As utilities begin to offer smart energy programs and services, it is important to understand that their customers have already downloaded billions of applications that enormously impact every facet of their lives. Customer service models built on call centers, automated phone attendants, and web pages are no longer enough as customers find their always-present mobile devices enable them to find immediate solutions and gratification. Untethered connectivity is transforming consumers' definition of customer experience excellence.

In their book of the same name, authors Ted Schadler, Josh Bernoff, and Julie Ask describe the transformation as *The Mobile Mind Shift*:

> You can actually see the mobile mind shift as it happens. First, people get a smartphone. They start using it. They increase the frequency with which they interact, and the diversity of locations. They download apps. They begin to expect, and then demand, mobile services from companies they deal with. And they move through stages—first communicating, then consuming content, and finally transacting.[14]

Utilities must understand that their customers expect connected services because they're already receiving them from most everyone else they do business with. The bar for what constitutes basic service has risen because of the level of smart services they're already receiving elsewhere. It is becoming commonplace for consumers, through an untethered digitally connected device, to manage every facet of their life, from anywhere, at any time. It's a phenomenon I will refer to throughout this book as "mobility."

When Amazon, FedEx, and UPS can push information to all my connections, updating me on the status of their delivery, why can't my utility tell me about the status of my outage restoration? When DIRECTV allows me through a smartphone app to set any of the digital video recorders in my house from anywhere in the world, why must I call the utility and have them send an employee to my house to turn on, off, or transfer my service? When with a few swipes of my finger I can load money onto my smartphone Starbucks app and buy coffee and have the balance updated in real time, why does it take hours for my utility to post my payment?

Lee Willis, of Quanta Technology, said it best in a Greentech Media article: "If your smartphone can tell you where the closest sushi bar is, and then tell you if your friends are already there, and then you can check your bank balance to see if you can buy the first round of drinks, then just having your smart meter shave a little off peak demand is not good enough."[15]

Digital devices, ubiquitous connectivity, and the mobile computing they enable are disrupting the customer experience. Their impact is not linear but exponential.

Michael Saylor stated in his book *The Mobile Wave*:

> It's easy to fall into the trap of assuming that a new technology is very similar to its predecessors. A new technology is often perceived as the linear extension of the previous one, and this leads us to believe the new technology will fill the same roles—just a little faster or a little smaller or a little lighter.

Yet every now and again, a truly *disruptive* technology appears and causes major changes to business, society, or economics. It yields nonlinear effects on so many levels and at such a grand scale that it's very hard to grasp the scope until after the dust settles.

Mobile computing is this type of disruptive technology.[16]

Or as Saylor pointed out more succinctly and very powerfully: "Whenever teenage girls and corporate CEOs covet the same new technology, something extraordinary is happening."[17]

Or to shamelessly adapt Saylor's quote based on watching my 3- and 6-year-old granddaughters grow: "Whenever your grandchildren can embrace and navigate technology before they can talk, something extraordinary is happening."

The speed of this personal technology revolution will continue to accelerate and recalibrate the lens the consumer uses to judge the customer experience. It is not a linear evolution. It is a disruptive revolution. Even though this change is only a few years old, we live as if this transformation in how we live, work, and play have been around for generations. We are beginning to be very comfortable with this new technology and thus fall into the trap that the future for these connected technologies will be linear—a little faster, a little better smartphone or tablet, with more games and apps.

The transformation of the last few years has been driven primarily by smartphones and tablets, which combine a lot of capabilities into one device. But we are on the verge of another major disruptive phase driven by omnipresent digital communication. It is commonly referred to as the "Internet of Things," where all devices will be connected. We will see a proliferation of capabilities across a whole new set of devices and platforms: wearable tech, quantified self, artificial intelligence, virtual agents, digital wallets, connected cars, and connected homes. Plus we will see a convergence in how the consumer lives across these platforms.

This continued acceleration in the consumer adoption of connected technologies will continue to drive new innovations in the customer experience. The change will not be linear. It will be disruptive.

The question for utilities as their customers get smarter is, "How smart will you be?"

CHAPTER 3

How Smart Will You Be?

THE CONTRASTS ARE STARTLING

The black and white picture on the top is from over 50 years ago. I'm the cute one in the middle between the two evil older brothers. If you look closely, you'll see I'm holding a pair of binoculars. Like smartphones today, it was the tech toy of its age that fathers let their kids hold and play with. I thought I was pretty cool because I could see down the street.

The picture on the bottom of page 13 is of my grand-daughter when she was 2-and-a-half-years old. She is naturally comfortable in the operation of a laptop, an iPhone, and an iPad. In the term coined by Marc Prensky,[18] she is a digital native. In other words, my granddaughter was born into a world of wirelessly connected digital mobile devices.

I was cool because I could see down the street. My grand-daughter is really cool because she can, at anytime and any-place, access the whole world, and see it, and talk to it, because she is always connected, always on.

I can't think of a bigger contrast between the two pictures. The difference in the degree of connectivity and what it means for how people live is off the charts.

However, for utilities, the contrast is not dramatically different. In my childhood, over 50 years ago, when the utility wanted to read your meter, they walked by it. Today, the majority of meters still require you to walk by them, or at least drive by them. Fifty years ago when a customer needed to initiate service, the utility dispatched a utility worker to go to the meter and turn it on. Today, the majority of utilities still work that way. Fifty years ago when a customer's power went out they had to call the utility to inform them they had a problem. Today, the customer still must call. Fifty years ago a utility customer had only a couple of rate options. Today, most consumers only have one or two pricing options.

There is a lack of contrast in the utility aspects of my illustrations because connectivity has not been applied to the grid to the extent it has been applied to the consumer. I'm not trying to throw stones here. In fairness to utilities, most of these connected capabilities are less than 10 years old. Plus, some utilities *are* moving in the right direction by making massive capital commitments to smart grid and beginning to change the services provided to their customers. But the point is that utilities are at a critical juncture: How, and at what speed, will utilities respond to the dramatic changes in their connected customers' expectations?

THIS TIME IS DIFFERENT

As utilities think through how to respond they need to realize today is very different from their past experiences with customer care innovation. I began in the '70s when the key customer service tool was microfiche. In the '80s, we put the microfiche and customer information systems online. In the '90s, the digital phone switch enabled 1-800 number centralized call centers. The web in the 2000s enabled electronic billing and payment.

Historically, it has been a paced progression of corporations delivering customer service innovations. But this decade is very different. For the first time we're seeing the changes on the customer's side. And this makes the changes in customer service no longer under the corporation's paced and linear control. It means consumers are in control. And they're disruptive.

Brad Cleveland in his book *Call Center Management on Fast Forward* said:

> We are now seeing a major and fundamental shift: For the first time, developments on the customer's side of the equation—the meteoric rise of smartphones, social media, broadband, and mobility—are the most significant factors driving customer expectations and services. Given what is happening, I'm convinced we'll see more change in the next five years than we've seen in the past two decades. We can harness and leverage the trends to our benefit, or we can get tumbled by them. We're entering the new era of customer relationships.[19]

Where your customers live, how they live, and the time-table upon which they live, are changing drastically and rapidly. Incremental change in how utilities interact with their untethered, connected customers will only leave them further behind and further isolated.

To provide the experiences their customers will be demanding, utilities must begin the journey now to create a substantial leap in their customer interaction capabilities. To determine how smart they must be, utilities must understand how wireless digital connectivity has impacted their customers and the opportunities it presents. In Chapter 4, "The New Consumer," I cover the dramatic changes creating a very different consumer. Then in Chapter 5, "From Back-of-Mind to Engagement and Relationships," I cover what I believe is the biggest opportunity for utilities presented by consumer mobility: to engage their customers and build relationships.

The New Consumer: Me, Myself & I

TECHNOLOGY IS THE ENABLER

The transformation in the technology serving consumers and being used by consumers has created tremendous growth in the service-channel options that companies offer their customers: voice call, interactive voice response, speech recognition, artificial intelligence, web, text messaging, mobile applications, social media. Additionally, the growth in the devices consumers use to connect to those who serve them has experienced tremendous growth. Historically, the primary connection to my product and service provider was my landline phone, cellular phone, or PC. Today, these interaction platforms are expanding to a host of additional options: smartphone, tablet, phablet, smart watch, smart thermostat, quantified self, connected car. As stated earlier, another major aspect of this technology transformation is mobility. Omnipresent wireless connectivity has had a tremendous impact on the immediacy in which consumers and companies can interact with each other.

Because this technology is dramatically changing how consumers connect and interact with those they buy products and services from, it is only natural that much of the buzz and hype be about these new consumer technologies. However, I think the customer care transformation is less about the technology and more about the consumer. Focusing on channel, smart, and mobility is technology-centric and is not adequate for capturing the consumers' perspective.

There is a technology transformation underway, and technology is a key enabler of the customer care transformation. But focusing on the technology misses the changes occurring in the consumer.

THE DIFFERENCE IS THE CONSUMER

Prior technological revolutions that impacted consumers were primarily single dimensional: The phone made calls. The radio and television informed and entertained. The 8-track, cassette, and CD player played songs.

This technological revolution created by ubiquitous, digitally connected devices is drastically different from anything before because it enables a diverse and wide array of things that are changing every aspect of how people live, work, and play. Consider the scads of smartphone apps providing services across all facets of the human existence: Since the release of Apple iOS, 1.2 million-plus apps have been downloaded more than 75 billion times,[20] and Android's over 1.3 million apps are downloaded 1 billion times a month.[21]

And it's impacting everybody—not just the younger Millennial or Generation Y demographics. It's cross-demographic. Brian Solis, author of the book *The End of Business as Usual*, calls these connected customers Generation C:

> The connected customer is the stranger you must get to know. In comparison to the customers of the past, this group is only growing and it's traversing demographics. Nowadays, age ain't

nothing but a number. It is how people embrace technology, from social networks to smartphones to intelligent appliances, that contributes to the digital lifestyle that is now synonymous with Gen-C.[22]

Digital devices and ubiquitous connectivity mean the consumer is always connected, always on. This personal connectivity means intimacy. Phone numbers and addresses that used to denote a place now represent a specific person because cellphones and smartphones are personal and always near you. Research firm Pew Internet reports two-thirds of cellphone owners sleep with or near their cellphone.[23] A study by integrated marketing agency 11mark called *IT in the Toilet* reported three-fourths of Americans with mobile phones have used them in the bathroom.[24] When was the last time your cellphone was not close by? Or the last time you left home or the office without your smartphone? Your smartphone is always with you and represents only you.

This personal and intimate connectivity with a significant computing platform enables companies to transform the customer experiences they provide and significantly change how customers interact with them. It is this change in the customer experience, through intimate connectivity, that significantly raises the bar. It has created spoiled customers, who expect superior, personalized service anyplace, anytime, instantaneously.

Customer contact used to mean get in the car and drive to the store, or write a letter and put it in the mailbox, or go to your home landline phone and make a call. Each required a relatively large degree of effort and a certain degree of inconvenience, especially if the lines and hold times were long. Things got a little easier with the Internet, which enabled people to get connected through their PCs or Macs. But this still required effort to go to your computer, boot-up, and log-on to interact with a company. Today, because I'm always connected and always on, I have the ability at my fingertips to contact a company and solve complex problems easily and instantaneously.

By planting their applications directly on their customers' devices, companies are causing a shift in the customer experience by meeting needs and solving problems in ways that weren't previously possible. Once customers experience these new possibilities, it creates a different set of expectations for an excellent customer experience. It is this different set of expectations that is key. It's not about being able to say "we have an app for that." It's about meeting a different set of individual customer expectations that are created by an always-connected, always-on device that is at my fingertips and always available to do something for me right now.

THE NEW CONSUMER: ME, MYSELF & I

This new set of grand customer expectations is the significant disruption in customer care. It is creating a new consumer I call, "Me, Myself & I."

Because many companies are enabling consumers to immediately access them and conveniently launch an inquiry, execute a transaction, or resolve a complex problem, consumers have an ever-increasing level of expectations: Consumers who can do anything, at any time, and at any place expect companies to do the same.

It also creates a customer who is as intelligent as you about your products and services—including your flaws, scars, and warts. Connectivity and access to vast social and knowledge networks means a large number of consumers know your systems and processes by accessing your customers' opinions of their experiences with you. In other words, your customers are educated about you by the time they contact your company, so they're better informed and have higher expectations. Bottom line, they expect your company to be smart too.

Because of this connectivity, consumers increasingly want it all—and they want it now. Historically acceptable call center customer experience metrics—an average speed of answer (ASA) of less than 60 seconds, an average handle time of less than 240 seconds, and a first-contact resolution greater than 80 percent—are dramatically different for the Me, Myself & I customer. On a mobile application, they expect an ASA of immediately, an average handle time of a few swipes of the finger, and a first-contact resolution of 100 percent. If your app doesn't do this, they will not return.

This new mobility has shifted the power in customer service from the corporation to the consumer. Today's consumers have the power to influence what the vast social community thinks of your company and its products. If they believe your company or its products have wronged them, they have the power to take their case to the social media community. If the community believes the customer has a case, they will spread that case virally across the planet for the world to be judge, jury, and executioner. The information that impacts the consumers' perceptions and actions now comes predominantly from the social community and not from the corporation.

One can argue that it has always been about serving your customers. But there is a key difference here: The power has shifted to the consumer. Not just to consumers as a group but, more important, to the individual consumer. This is why I use multiple descriptors of the individual—Me, Myself & I—to denote the exponential power that is now centered and emanating from the individual. Any way you cut it, from any angle, the only perceptions that matter now lie with this new consumer—Me, Myself & I. The individual is now in control and holds the power in forming perceptions regarding your product, service, and company. Me, Myself & I decide what they pay attention to and how they respond. They are no longer powerless and captive to accept what you give them. This is your new consumer—one who views their customer care experience from the perspective of "Are you doing anything for Me, Myself & I?"

SCREW THE COMMUNITY. . .THIS IS ABOUT ME!

The term "social media" has risen to buzzword status by being applied across many things without consistent definition and understanding. The context for social I'm applying here is in terms of consumers using social technologies to influence opinion and reputations. In their book *Groundswell: Winning in a World Transformed by Social Technologies,* authors Charlene Li and Josh Bernoff describe it as "a spontaneous movement of people using online tools to connect, take charge of their own experience, and get what they need—information, support, ideas, products, and bargaining power—from each other. Simply put, groundswell is a social trend in which people use technologies to get the things they need from each other instead of from companies."[25]

The power and impact of social media on companies' brand, image, marketing, and communications cannot be overemphasized. Historically, corporate marketing and communications departments were the main source of product information, but that has been replaced by social media. Utilities have generally embraced social media because they understand the need to monitor and participate in online social community conversations. It presents huge opportunities for customers to be educated on all things smart grid and smart energy. It has the potential to create communities that are excited and tell others about the good things smart grid and smart energy provides. Outage communication has been significantly improved using social media.

However, it is important that utilities do not confuse the branding, image, communication, and educational aspects of social media with customer service. In my opinion, social media should not be used as a major platform for customer service. Social is part of today's customer experience, but people are making too big a leap by seeing social media as a great channel for customer service, contact, and interaction. It has application to the customer experience, but it should not to be a main delivery channel for customer service.

Social media is about the community. Customer service is about Me, Myself & I. The community is important when consumers want to know what people they trust are thinking or when they want to spread the word on an issue of importance to them. It's a good channel for communication to the masses. But when a consumer is receiving service from a company, it is about Me, Myself & I.

Onstar is a good example. Onstar is the capability within GM cars to have a direct link to a concierge, providing services ranging from directions to emergency response. Facebook and Twitter are good platforms for forming a community to share their experiences with Onstar. They are also great channels for Onstar to communicate helpful information to their customers, such as automobile maintenance, safety, and security tips. But when I lock my keys in my car, the community is not going to solve my problem. Telling the community I locked my keys in my car might relieve some frustration, but it won't unlock my door. I don't want to wait around to see if the community is monitored and hope that someone at Onstar will initiate a command to unlock my door.

The power of ubiquitous connectivity for resolving issues is not that I can access Facebook or Twitter's site and take my problems to the community. It is that I can access a smartphone application that enables Me, Myself & I to immediately have Onstar unlock my door.

Great social media competencies will not overcome a company with poor or limited customer service channels. When I have a problem, it's about Me, Myself & I—and when it is about me, I need a customer service channel that can take care of me immediately. People use the social community for customer service when the company's service has failed them or has not provided easy and convenient solutions on the platforms where they live, work, and play. If you are having a lot of customer care traffic on your social media channels, it is likely a sign that your core customer service processes are broken. You don't want to use increased customer service traffic on Facebook and Twitter as a measure of success. There are many other new mobility-enabled channels that are better suited to provide an excellent customer service experience for the new consumer. I will cover these in more detail in later chapters.

THE OPPORTUNITY: INTIMATE DIRECT ENGAGEMENT

The huge customer service opportunity is not the access to social communities but an opportunity for a direct real-time connection to individual customers to tailor interactions to each one of them. Connectivity has made it easy to form, access, and communicate with communities who share like-minded interests. Connectivity has also enabled new customer service options to be delivered to customers. However, this common connectivity does not make social and customer service one in the same.

What is transformational about connectivity's impact on customer service is that it enables affordable increased service, interaction, and engagement tailored to the needs and preferences of each customer. Companies no longer need to depend on broad communications to masses of their customers. They can now tailor interactions and communications to Me, Myself & I based on the specific preferences each customer has established for specific conditions.

It is not about the community. It is not about a group of call types. It is not about a group of contacts by channel. It is about the ability to provide exceptional customer interactions, across many channels and devices, specifically tailored to your new consumer: Me, Myself & I.

CHAPTER 5

From Back-of-Mind to Engagement and Relationship

GREAT IS NOT GOOD ENOUGH

In 2000, the National Academy of Engineering (NAE) named "Electrification—the vast networks of electricity that power the developed world"—as the number-one engineering impact of the 20th century. The NAE noted that electrification "powers almost every pursuit and enterprise in modern society," and it has "literally lighted the world and impacted countless areas of daily life, including food production and processing, air conditioning and heating, refrigeration, entertainment, transportation, communication, health care, and computers."[26]

For over a century, the utility industry has done a marvelous job of providing a product that is reliable, safe, affordable, ubiquitous, and delivered instantaneously. It is almost always there when we flip the switch or when an appliance calls for it.

As wonderful as electricity is, customers are not actively engaged with its consumption. It is a product that is unseen and provides no context for the amount being consumed. The consumption comes from engagement with appliances and devices that consume the electricity, not with the kilowatt itself.

Since there has been little direct engagement with electricity consumption, the majority of interaction between utility and customer has been around the bare necessities. In between the sporadic move, the occasional outage, and the monthly billing cycle, there has been no need for utilities to want a customer to think about them. In fact, I've heard a number of utility executives utter the phrase, "We're doing our best work when customers don't need to think about us." The nature of the physics of electricity, combined with how it is consumed and utilities' focus on the reliable delivery of the commodity has created a product that is "back-of-mind" for most customers. And for the most part, everybody has been very comfortable with it generally being invisible most of the time.

As a result, consumers have not associated a conscious value or relationship with the product. Hence the ever-present unfairness of people happily waiting in line at Starbucks to pay close to $5 for a latte, yet complaining about their electric bill that averages much less per day for electrons that are delivered instantaneously.

In my opinion, electricity is the killer app of all killer apps. Yet if you were to ask consumers, where would they rate electricity, the answer would probably not be very high. Just imagine what the electric industry might look like today if Apple founder Steve Jobs or Starbucks founder Howard Schultz had been leading it.

In a century where electric utilities built the most marvelous of engineering achievements, they focused on the delivery of the commodity and not the relationship with the customer.

What may likely be this century's greatest achievement—digital connectivity—presents utilities a significant new opportunity. Not just to deliver a smarter commodity, but also to engage energy consumers in ways that create a deep and valuable relationship between the utility and their customer.

THE NEED FOR A RELATIONSHIP

Why is a relationship with your customer important now if it wasn't critical in the previous century? For one, it impacts your return on equity (ROE). According to a study by J.D. Power and Associates, those in the top quartile for customer satisfaction one year before a rate case receive a .5 percent increment increase in ROE compared to those in the bottom quartile.[27]

For another, the consumer has unparalleled power because connectivity has created the ability to reach vast social networks and communities. Because of the Internet's reach and speed, ignore your customers, and you risk being taken to the social media town square for a public stoning.[28]

Another is that utilities now need to influence how and when consumers use energy. Previously, utilities mostly focused on putting the energy on the grid. Now, utilities play a critical role in changing how and when energy is consumed. If utilities, in managing their power grid supply, are going to count on consumers' demand reduction with as much confidence as other physical power-generation sources, then utilities must be able to engage the consumer, and more important, sustain their engagement. You cannot influence consumers and sustain a change unless you have a relationship with them.

Without a relationship, delivering a perfect product is not good enough and will doom utilities to the fate of the airlines. Like utilities, the airline industry provides an engineering marvel by enabling hundreds of thousands of people each day to be transported safely across the globe at over 500 miles an hour. Yet in the airlines' focus on safely moving planes at high speeds from one city to another, they have become disconnected from their customer. By any reasonable measure, people should be very happy with airlines for getting them safely and affordably to their destination faster than any other mode of transportation and better than any other generation has been able to travel. But because of an inability to deliver consistently the softer side of their product—care and comfort[29]—the airline industry is routinely rated at the bottom of the American Customer Satisfaction Index.[30]

Utilities cannot just focus on what they've always done—building the most reliable and marvelous system of delivering electricity. In our connected world where almost every aspect of daily life is powered by electricity, any power outage—no matter how minor, justified, or due to an act of God—is no longer something consumers let roll off their backs. Throwing all the utility's resources at doing a superb job of restoration is no longer enough. The same act of God that has me mad as hell because the airline delayed my flight and can't tell me my options also has me mad when I finally get home to find my house without power and the utility unable to tell me my estimated time of restoration. Customers now expect care, empathy, and communication as part of their restoration experience.[31]

And it's not just the customer expectations for outage reporting and restoration. Utilities must use the capabilities of a digital grid to deliver new consumer products. Utilities struggling with engaging their customers with smart energy will not be allowed to retreat to their comfort zone by applying digital technology to just the grid and stopping at the meter. Consumers will demand more than just a commodity reliably delivered to the meter.

This is evidenced in the pushback utilities are receiving from customers as they receive smart grid, smart meters, smart energy, big data, and increased rates. Customers are asking, "What's in it for me?" Utilities spending billions of dollars without delivering new products, programs, and services the customers value, is from the consumer perspective, asking them to pay more for what they already get.

As customers become increasingly digitally connected, their expectations of an excellent customer experience will continue to exponentially rise. A reliable, safe, and affordable commodity is no longer enough. Utilities must become consumer product companies. This means they must engage their customers and build relationships.

We can doom ourselves to the fate of the airlines, or we can seize the opportunity to reinvent ourselves into a customer relationship industry.

THE NEW COMPETITIVE THREAT

Even though the utilities' retail transaction may be within a regulated monopoly, the insertion of other parties into the process of providing energy information and control will make it even more difficult to build customer relationships. Typically industry pundits see energy storage and distributed generation as the likely technologies that enable utility bypass. I believe the more immediate risk is bypassing the utility for energy information and control. Utilities need to engage their customers to change their behavior, and, therefore, their demand on the grid, so it is critical customers look first to the utility for energy information and control. The challenge is there are now numerous companies that are inserting themselves between the utility and their customers.

The Nest thermostat, developed by Apple alumni, is a connected, smart digital device that boosts energy efficiency and provides a key source of information and control for a customer's heating and cooling. Nest has a nationally scaled platform that provides its customers with unprecedented control and information. With this home-connected device, Nest has complete access to information about its customer's lifestyle patterns, energy usage, and efficiency. Nest is now squarely between the utility and the customer for heating and cooling. And now Google is squarely between the utility and the customer with their $3.2 billion acquisition of Nest.

Additionally, Green Button is a program created in response to a call to action by the White House for utilities to provide consumers access to easy-to-understand information regarding their energy usage. Today, utilities serving 36 million customers provide a standard data interface that enables third parties to provide applications that use meter data to bring new energy usage and information services to their customers.[32] I acknowledge that the current method of getting your energy information from Green Button is not user-friendly. But over time, easy, friendly, and compelling utility usage, cost, and efficiency information and control from third parties will become commonplace. This is exactly what happened to banks when customers began using third-party software, such as Quicken, Mint, and iFinance, to aggregate the access of their banking, credit card, and brokerage information. A large percentage of customers never go to their financial services company online accounts because of the third-party tools available to aggregate their information and control.

In May 2013, Nest acquired MyUtility, an online service that aggregates all your utility usage and cost information in one place and evaluates it compared to similar homes.[33] A month later, at Apple's Worldwide Developers Conference (WWDC), the HomeKit developers' platform was released to provide an iOS-based protocol for connecting devices in the home. Then a month later, Nest introduced it's own wireless protocols called Thread.[34] A major significance of these open platforms is that they become a magnet for the brightest, most innovative, and highly creative people in the world. When developers can have immediate access to a global distribution channel, why would they develop anywhere else? Keep in mind that once developers have an app ready for release, they can access an Apple distribution channel that has over 800 million connected devices.

There is clearly a battle for information and control between the utility's online and paper reports and the third party's apps and online information. Few, if any, consumers will regularly interact with multiple sources. There will only be a few winners for the consumers' information and control. The one who makes it the easiest for the consumer to make a difference in their energy usage and cost will win the customer's relationship.

For those utilities that are deregulated or unbundled and believe being a transmission and distribution utility doesn't require new customer engagement and a deeper relationship, they only need to look at the customers' requirements for outage reporting and service restoration. J.D. Power and Associates 2014 *Electric Utility Residential Customer Satisfaction Study* reported a significant increase in overall satisfaction "when utilities proactively communicate outage information regularly and clearly via the channels customers prefer."[35]

It is no longer enough for a utility to do an outstanding job of restoring service after a storm. Customers are demanding utilities provide information regarding their outage and estimated time of restoration. The more extended an outage, the more they expect regular updates. Once power is restored, they expect the utility to follow up with them to verify the power has indeed been restored. Customers now consider this engagement a vital part of the process.[36]

In any case, a back-of-mind customer relationship is no longer adequate. Utilities can no longer build the grid and expect people to automatically accept it. It is critical that utilities move from a passive relationship to an active one with their always-connected, always-on, demanding, want-it-all-now, Me, Myself & I consumer.

OUTCOME-BASED CUSTOMER ENGAGEMENT

Smart energy, smart meters, smart grid, energy efficiency, demand response, pricing options, renewables, distributed generation, and customer service programs are driving the realization that consumers hold the key to success. Even though utilities have understood for some time that they have customers, not rate-payers, only recently have we begun to see the balance of power shift to the consumer. Utilities are realizing that any program's success is dependent on the consumer connecting in some way with their initiatives. Thus the latest beehive of buzzwords being attached to the word "customer": engagement, relationship, education, awareness, participation, experience, and communication. For our discussion here, I will lump them all under the term "customer engagement."

I propose a framework that not only clarifies the degree of customer engagement to aim for but also focuses on results. As utilities increase the resources dedicated to customer engagement, it is critical not to confuse activity with accomplishment. Success should be measured within the context of outcome-based customer engagement. All programs and services must be gauged on the level of customer engagement achieved, not on the program design or efforts.

There are four levels of customer engagement:

1. *Presentment:* These are messages and programs that are exposed to the consumer. They may or may not have been consciously seen, read, or heard. The key distinction is they were presented in some form to the consumer but not internalized for later recall.

2. *Awareness:* These are messages and programs that the consumer consciously saw, read, or heard and were placed in their memory. The key distinction is they can be recalled to some extent later as events trigger their memory.

3. *Action:* These are messages and programs that caused the consumer to take some action desired by the utility.

4. *Sustainability:* These are messages and programs that cause the consumer to repeatedly take some action desired by the utility.

Often messages are presented and not received as bill inserts get quickly tossed, bill messages become buried deep in the multiple-page granular detail, direct-mail energy reports become lost in a sea of junk mail, and tweets or Facebook posts are lost among a consumer's dozens of friends or followers. Utilities may be able to claim a high number of messages sent to a large number of people. But to what end? Presentment means you can check off the box for that activity, but you have not achieved a meaningful result with your customers.

Often mass communication can create a level of consciousness about the utility that was not there previously. Building a desired perception or understanding can have a positive impact. J.D. Power's studies routinely show a higher level of customer satisfaction when the consumer is aware of a utility's various programs and offerings. Their *2014 Consumer Engagement Study* reports those not aware of a utility's offerings average an overall customer satisfaction index of 587 compared to 646 for those aware of the offerings but not participating in any of them. Clearly achieving a level of awareness in your customer engagement efforts has an impact on overall customer satisfaction.

However, the study shows that the real return on investment is in the degree to which the utility achieves the action or sustainability level of customer engagement. On average, utilities whose customers are currently using one offering achieve an overall customer satisfaction score of 655; those using two achieve 682; three, 713; four, 747; and five or more a whopping 781. Clearly there are significant returns in getting customers to actively participate in utility programs and services.

The numbers also show a huge opportunity to increase the action and sustainability levels of customer engagement. J.D. Power's study reports that 77 percent of respondents were aware of at least one utility program or service. Of these, only 34 percent were participating in at least one of the 30 programs and services.

Thirty-four percent may sound like a good outcome, but the data shows the biggest participation is for receiving an e-bill (21.5 percent), and in second place, the level or equal pay plan (5.7 percent). The other 28 programs and services fall at or below 3 percent participation levels. So outside of the standard electronic billing and budget bill programs, only 3 percent of utilities' customers, on average, are taking advantage of a program or service beyond just receiving the delivered commodity. However, there are huge opportunities to increase the level of participation: 20 percent use one utility program; 7 percent, two; 3 percent, three; 1 percent, four; and 2 percent, five or more.[37]

Achieving action and sustainability in your customer engagement efforts brings into play a new dynamic not present in presentment and awareness. This new dynamic is the realization that the power of success ultimately resides in the hands of the consumer. A company can achieve presentment with millions of messages and with enough repetition that they eventually impact awareness. But to get the customer to take action and achieve sustainability means you must connect with the consumer on a level that is important to them. The old adage of "you can lead a horse to water, but you can't make him drink" is a rule that applies to outcome-based customer engagement. It is motivating the customer to take action that creates a meaningful return on your investment. Success must be measured not by your efforts, programs, and messages, but by the degree to which you motivate the customer to take action, and ideally, to continually repeat that changed behavior. As utilities begin to engage their customers, it is critical that leadership frame their measures of success in terms of accomplishment and not activity.

PART II

Rethink

CHAPTER 6

Relationship Prerequisites

NEW REQUIREMENTS FOR EVERY INTERACTION

The need to engage consumers and build a long-term relationship brings with it a new set of customer service prerequisites and requirements. It is one thing to enroll or acquire a customer for a one-time interaction; it's another thing if you want that customer to continue to interact and engage with you. Sustaining a behavior over a long period of time is a critical distinction in your customer care planning and design requirements because it presents an entirely different set of customer expectations you must meet.

There are three key prerequisites of service in order to engage the customer and sustain the engagement to the relationship level:

1. Do something for Me, Myself & I.

2. Make it easy.

3. Make the delivery flawless.

DO SOMETHING FOR ME, MYSELF & I

There is a point of view in this industry that customers don't want to engage with smart energy. I believe we are missing the point. It's not that they don't want to engage; it's that we are not providing anything the customer perceives as worthy of their time, money, or attention. Maybe we're ignoring the customer rather than them ignoring us?

Customers do indeed value and want affordable, reliable, convenient, and safe energy. That's what customers have always wanted and what utilities have always delivered. Now utilities want customers to pay higher rates for a smart grid, smart meter, and smart energy, plus they want customers to embrace the behavior changes required to help improve the grid.

However, customers are not receiving an answer to their question, "What's in it for Me, Myself & I?" In effect, we're telling them we are going to deliver the equivalent of the iPhone of energy, but we are packaging it as "sign up now for a 10-year contract and begin paying for the contract now. In return, we'll give you basically the same phone you have today, and five to 10 years down the road, we'll bring you some really cool apps." So what the customer hears is "pay me now, and you'll love what we deliver years later." It doesn't work that way if you need customers to be excited and engaged in what you're offering.

A key part of a relationship is that it is "two-way." Getting customers to listen, understand, and engage begins with them believing you have their best interests at heart. Having customers do something that is important to you requires you to also be doing things that are important to them.

I don't buy into the theory that customers have no interest to engage with their utilities. If that is true, why are there millions of calls going into utility call centers? Many will argue that it is because customers have problems or issues they need the utility to resolve. Exactly! So why are we not focusing smart energy, digitalization, and mobility on keeping these problems or issues from developing in the first place? For example, in a recent 12-month period, Salt River Project (SRP), an Arizona utility that serves 1 million customers, sent 16.7 million email messages and 900,000 text messages to its customers. These messages are tailored to each customer who signed up to receive proactive notifications for credit cycle alerts, time-of-use reminders, bill estimates, threshold alerts, and real-time payments and outage notifications. SRP is seeing a reduction in the calls to its call centers and is forming sustained relationships because it's using these new technologies to do things that are important to its customers.[38]

In our jump to engage customers with the equivalent of the "iPhone of energy," I think we have missed that there are a number of basic needs our customers have where they would welcome engagement. My first cellular phone, which was leading edge in its day, had a large handset with a big heavy cord connected to hardware in a canvas bag that plugged into my car's cigarette lighter. Even though my "bag phone" was heavy and clunky and not at all cutting edge by today's standards, I was very happy with it because it eliminated a basic pain point: It enabled me to make an affordable mobile call. In our zeal to roll out a more intelligent grid and promise a future of smart energy, we are missing opportunities to eliminate basic customer pain points. Digitization and connectivity brings a wealth of opportunities for eliminating the pain points associated with establishing service, the monthly mystery bill, budget billing, billing accuracy, deposits, payment posting, credit arrangements, and appointments. I'll outline this in more detail throughout Section II. But a prerequisite for engagement and relationship is that you solve Me, Myself & I's problems and fulfill their needs.

MAKE IT EASY

In the *Harvard Business Review* article "To Keep Your Customers, Keep It Simple," Patrick Spenner and Karen Freeman examine what makes consumers "sticky." In other words, what makes consumers likely to follow through on a purchase, make repeat purchases, and tell others to buy the product? Spenner and Freeman found "the single biggest driver of stickiness, by far, was 'decision simplicity'—the ease with which consumers can gather trustworthy information about a product and confidently and efficiently weigh their purchase options."[39]

In *The Persistence of Consumer Choice*, a case study prepared by Judith Schwartz of To the Point, a strategic marketing consultancy, a top lesson learned was "make the process easy and pleasant—nothing onerous—and let customers out of the programs if they change their minds at any point."[40]

The impact of simplicity is demonstrated by SRP's success with time-of-use (TOU) rate adoption and retention. SRP has 31 percent of their residential customers on one of four TOU rate options.[41] SRP gives customers who are switching to TOU a ninety-day money-back guarantee. If at the end of three months they've paid more than they would have on the standard rate, they'll refund the difference and put the customer back on their previous rate plan. Customers can easily see how they're doing because their bills indicate what their TOU bill is compared to what it would have been on the standard rate.[42]

Many believe one of the key prerequisites to engaging customers in smart energy is education. By educating consumers on the need for smart energy, we will get them to support, accept, and engage. Education certainly has a role, but it is a "push strategy" that will be a long and costly uphill journey. When I think of education to change consumers' behavior, I always think of stop-smoking campaigns. Over the last 50 years, we have spent billions of dollars to tell one of the most logical and compelling stories ever told on the need for behavior change. And just now are we seeing smokers become a minority. The reason it took a long time is not because we didn't have a compelling story, good communication, or adequate resources. It was because stopping smoking, and sustaining that behavior change, is a very hard thing to do. Knowledge does not always equal engagement or behavior change.

If you were thinking of committing significant resources to education, I would recommend you first look at how easy the process is. You can do all the education in the world, but if it isn't simple, the customer is unlikely to adopt. More important, your customer is very unlikely to sustain their adoption or behavior change.

Easy trumps education every time. You have to first make sure you have designed the program and customer interface with simplicity and ease in mind. In the words of SRP's customer service guiding principle, "make it rewarding, easy, and pleasant to do business with."[43]

MAKE THE DELIVERY FLAWLESS

Customers just want their need fulfilled or problem resolved. More and more customers prefer self-service because of its potential to conveniently and easily complete a transaction or resolve a problem.

The problem with self-service is that it exposes your process flaws directly to the customer. Often customer service representatives know where the potholes are in the process and can, behind the scenes, navigate the customer around them. But with self-service, from the customer's perspective, it either worked or didn't. And if it didn't work, they will then likely go to your most expensive channel: the customer service representative. Or worse yet, say negative things about you on social media.

The prerequisite for flawless execution becomes even more problematic when you want a customer to adopt new programs such as TOU rates, electronic bill and payment, usage alerts, and payment reminders. If the digital experience fails, your customers will quit paying attention to the messages, stop using the app, or quit the service altogether. A recent study by ClickFox, a software company providing journey-based analytics, indicated there is no loyalty when a mobile app fails. More than half will delete the application and visit the website instead. Only 4 percent would take the time to contact the call center.[44] In effect, they tried you, it failed, and they won't be back. Unfortunately, you won't even know it or have the chance to rectify it.

In this day of multichannel service, it is critical that your processes execute flawlessly in order to sustain engagement with your customers.

CHAPTER 7

Working for Me

RELIABILITY AND OUTAGE: TWO DISTINCT EXPERIENCES

In rethinking service for our digital world, we need to separate reliability from outage because they are two very different customer experiences. Reliability is very back-of-mind, whereas outage is very front-of-mind. In this chapter, we will cover reliability, and in the next chapter, "My Restoration," we will discuss outages.

RELIABILITY: THE UTILITY'S WORD, NOT THE CUSTOMER'S

A unique aspect of electricity, natural gas, and water delivery is reliability. We expect the product to be there when we flip the switch, when the furnace calls for it, or when we turn the faucet. As I mentioned earlier, utilities have done such a great job with continuous delivery that it is back-of-mind for customers. It has come to be expected, and little value is given for near-perfect delivery.

U.S. electricity reliability is excellent. Reliability data varies and is not widely available for all utilities. But generally the data would indicate that the average customer experiences less than two distribution system outages a year and is without power for around two hours per year.

The investments being made in smart grid will continue to improve reliability. Distribution automation will reroute power and reduce the number affected by an outage. Improved reporting information from smart meters and smart distribution devices will improve the information operations managers have and, therefore, speed restoration. There is no doubt that connecting digital communication to the grid is going to improve reliability.

But customers don't think in terms of reliability. Just like air, they don't think about it until it is missing. In the J.D. Power and Associates *Smart Energy Consumer Behavioral Segmentation Study*, text analytics was performed on a series of open-ended questions regarding smart grid. Interestingly, reliability was not a widely used word by the survey respondents. The report said, "It would appear that the industry delivers such a high degree of reliability that customers only think of reliability when something goes wrong. Therefore, their experience and appreciation isn't in terms of reliability and 'keeping the lights on,' but rather is in the context of 'when the lights go out.'"[45]

Reliability is the key mission of utilities, but it is not how customers define and evaluate the product nor is it how the customer puts context around the electricity product. Outage is how customers consciously experience your product, or lack thereof. Therefore, don't expect your customers to notice or give you any points for improved reliability because, under current service models, they won't be able to perceive the improvements. And that's the rub. Utilities do a marvelous job of continuously and reliably delivering a product and are on the path to making it even better, but their customers will never know it.

UNPERCEIVABLE IMPROVEMENT

The Illinois legislature passed a bill that allows the state's two largest utilities to build a smart grid and earn a return on the investment by increasing customers' bills by about $3 a month. The smart grid plan is tied to numerous performance measures. One of the criteria is that, over a 10-year period, utilities will have to reduce the number of outages by 20 percent and the duration of these outages by 15 percent.[46] Attaining these goals is a significant improvement in reliability and a return on the customer's investment in a smarter grid. But it is an improvement that customers will not perceive or appreciate on their own.

For example, a utility reducing System Average Interruption Frequency Index (SAIFI) from 2 to 1.6 events and System Average Interruption Duration Index (SAIDI) from 120 minutes to 102 minutes is a significant systemwide engineering accomplishment. But no matter how much you've improved your SAIDI and SAIFI, the first major storm that results in a multi-day outage will still result in customer angst and anger. A product, whose reliability is 99.8 percent, cannot expect customers to experience small fractional improvements.

A NEW CONTEXT

This is not to say that distribution automation and other smart grid investments aren't important or a good value for the consumer. But because of the consumer's inability to perceive improvements, utilities need to create a new context for reliability with their customers. Let me illustrate with examples from other industries that create a customer awareness of product reliability.

I pay $99 a year for Amazon Prime to have their goods delivered to me in two business days or less with no shipping fees. They send me a text when the order is shipped, on the day it is out on the local truck for delivery, and after it has been delivered to my home. They want me to be aware of the quality, reliability, and speed of their delivery. They also are making sure I realize they have fulfilled or beat their promised delivery schedule.

OnStar sends monthly vehicle diagnostics reports to its customers, detailing engine and transmission system, emissions system, air bag system, anti-lock braking system, tire pressure, and what general maintenance is due.[47] Rather than only thinking about your car when it breaks down, GM regularly reports, month after month, the car's reliability to the customer. Or in hopes of avoiding a breakdown, alerts you when it looks like your car may be developing a problem. OnStar keeps reliability front-of-mind as opposed to allowing you to only think of it when your car breaks down.

Florida Power & Light Company (FPL) serves approximately 4.6 million customers in Florida. FPL sets a great example for rethinking reliability, by taking communication to the Me, Myself & I level. Their website has a feature called, "System Improvements Near You," where customers can put in their address and see what improvements have been made near them. The infrastructure improvements listed include utility pole inspections, power line inspection with infrared technology, cleared vegetation from neighborhood power lines, cleared vegetation from main power lines, strengthened main power lines, strengthened power lines serving critical facilities, and strengthened power lines serving main roads.[48]

FPL isn't just trying to get customers to understand reliability. They're getting them to understand how hard they're working on their customers' behalf to "make our infrastructure stronger every day, in good weather and bad."[49] That's something the customer can understand compared to a percentage improvement in SAIDI or SAIFI.

A utility using smart meter and smart grid information to diagnose and fix many problems before an outage occurs is absolutely realizing the benefits from big data. But their customers will not see how hard they are working for them to increase reliability unless the utility finds ways to let them know. For example, customers who experience a 90-minute planned outage to have a transformer replaced will see themselves as having an inconvenient outage. They will not know how hard you are working for them unless you help them understand that it was your intelligent systems that identified an upcoming transformer failure and enabled you to prevent them from experiencing a seven-hour equipment failure outage. A utility that is able to restore outages before the customer has to call will get no credit for timely response. The customer will come home and see his clock blinking and think poor reliability, not rapid response.

I suggest rethinking reliability along the lines of FPL but also to push the information to the customer. As part of your customer apps, provide the option to update customers through email or text on the improvements done in their area. I also think Distribution Management Systems (DMS) and Outage Management Systems (OMS) need the ability to update customers when a distribution automation device has just prevented a prolonged outage. Much like OnStar's maintenance report letting me know my car's systems are working, a text telling me the grid just rerouted power reminds me my utility is working for me.

The Smart Grid Consumer Collaborative report, *Consumer Voices*, found that one of the benefits with the greatest customer interest was improved reliability.[50] I agree when the subject is specifically presented to customers—they all want reliability. However, my point is that they won't naturally perceive reliability or its improvement on their own. You must let customers know specifically what you're doing to improve the system. Not just in broad public relations terms but also in granular specific terms tailored to Me, Myself & I. Make sure I know how hard you're working for me.

CHAPTER 8

My Restoration

A ROYAL PAIN-IN-THE-ASS

Customers demand near-perfect power as a base expectation. The study *Willingness to Pay to Avoid Outages: Reliability Demand Survey* by Bates White Economic Consulting, reports that 95 percent of respondents believe they should never experience an outage (58 percent) or they should be very rare (37 percent), except for those related to major storms or extreme weather. When they do have an outage, 66 percent of them experience significant problems if the outage lasts more than 12 hours, and 84 percent have significant problems if the outage lasts more than a day.[51]

Even though customers may be rational and understand there will be times a major storm causes extended outages, it causes them great inconvenience. So much inconvenience that they're willing to pay an extra $10 to $40 a month to never have an outage greater than four hours. Or another example, 62 percent of customers would find it unacceptable to have multiple outages per year lasting two days, even if they were paid $500 for each outage. Furthermore, 37 percent would not find it acceptable if they were paid $1,000 for each outage.[52]

There is a reason for this intolerance. Connectivity has changed the impact of outages on customers. Up until 10 years ago, the initial impact of an outage meant no TV. Your house would stay comfortable for hours, and refrigeration was not immediately impacted. Life went on comfortably for a number of hours. Today, outages means the always-connected, always-on customer is now *off*. This is best demonstrated in this excerpt from Stanley Bing's July 2012 *Fortune* magazine article, "A Cloudless Night." In it, Bing describes how in this day and age, the blackout he is experiencing means more than losing your lights:

> The TV was a doorstop. I don't have a transistor radio. My laptop had about a 50% charge. If I was careful that could last me … a couple of hours … I felt a rivulet of sweat on my brow. Of course there was no Internet. My Verizon box was down and with it my wireless network.
>
> I was sobbing softly as I went to my iPhone and tried to tweet out an SOS. My phone was dead! I had forgotten to charge it, and now it was too late! Too late! We assume that a good charge is only a wall plug away! But now it wasn't!
>
> I stood in my living room surrounded by the inert detritus of our digital cosmos. No Facebook! No Twitter! No Pinterest! No iTunes! No movies! No downloads! And, good God, no capacity to send or receive e-mail? I sank to my knees. No entertainment, no access to work, no social media. Just … me. I have never felt so alone. And then the lights went on.[53]

Bottom-line: Today's outages immediately impact how we live. The customer experience during an outage, and therefore their expectations, are very different today than 10 years ago.

TALK TO ME

J.D. Power and Associates, through their electric utility customer satisfaction surveys, has a wealth of data regarding the customers' expectations regarding outage reporting and service restoration. Their data consistently and clearly indicates higher satisfaction with those utilities that have committed to communicating with their customers regarding the outage and estimated time of restoration.

For example, utilities that provide four or more points of information to customers calling about their outage score significantly higher than those that provide only one or two points of information. The most critical information provided is the cause of the outage and an accurate estimated time of restoration.[54] Numerous utilities are using this data to improve their outage communication—specifically, its content, frequency, and delivery channel.

Companies such as Twenty-First Century Communications (TFCC) have significantly improved the outage communication experience by providing utilities with large capacity communications channels so customers can avoid getting a busy signal and report their outages via an automated phone attendant. On June 29, 2012, a "super derecho" moved at 75 mph for 700 miles from northern Indiana to the Southern Mid-Atlantic coast, causing 4.2 million customers to lose power. TFCC's infrastructure fielded 5.7 million inbound calls with 4 million received within just the first three days of the storm.[55]

Another example is iFactor, which improves the outage experience by providing utilities a web or mobile app channel for their customers to report an outage. During the same derecho, iFactor Storm Center mobile apps completed close to 700,000 customer transactions for Pepco, Atlantic City Electric, and Delmarva Power.[56]

Additionally, iFactor provides utilities the ability to show, on the web, tablet, or mobile platforms, a map of the outage location, the number of outage events, and the number of customers without power.

Over the last decade, utilities' mass communication during outages has improved. Corporate communications is now routinely involved in the operations meetings so the appropriate information can be released through the local media. In addition, this information is released through recordings that play when the customer calls about their outages and is also broadcast through Facebook and Twitter. Numerous utilities provide proactive outbound phone, email and text messages to update customers with outage and restoration information.

IT'S NOW ABOUT MY OUTAGE AND ME

Although the infrastructure for interacting with customers during massive outages has improved, numerous other service providers in other industries have also vastly improved the information they provide their customers. As a result, customer expectations for information during outages have outpaced utilities' improvement of the communication process.

For example, FedEx informs me about the delivery status of my package every step of the way. American Express immediately alerts me every time a charge is made without my physical credit card being present for the transaction. Smart Things sensors notify me if my garage door has been opened or closed or when it's been open for 30 minutes. Apple's Find My iPhone will pinpoint the location of my iPhone if I've lost it. So with everyone telling me substantial details about the service they provide, why can't a utility tell me any substantial detail about my outage and when my specific service will be restored?

In the initial hours following a major storm, customers may understand that you don't know details about restoration. Stating that the utility has already been notified of the outage and providing information about the total number of customers out and when the customer can expect to have the next update on restoration may suffice initially. But the clock quickly ticks away to the time that the customer demands information about their specific outage.

Every utility will experience their turn in the spotlight due to a major storm causing severe system damage, resulting in a large number of customers being out of power for multiple days. When it does, their regulatory relationships, political capital, corporate image, rate of return, and earnings per share will be at risk. And the elephant in the room is that increasingly, no matter how many resources you throw at the system damage or how much general communication you do, it will not be enough.

As Hurricane Sandy was approaching the Northeast, Massachusetts Governor Deval Patrick was asked if he expected utilities to be better prepared for this storm. The governor responded, "They better be." He went on to say, "People don't want to deal with their utilities being out for days at a time, but if it's going to be days at a time, they want to know it's days at a time and not 'we're going to have it up at midnight,' and midnight comes and goes and nothing happens."[57]

Four days after Hurricane Sandy, New York Governor Andrew Cuomo sent a letter to the CEOs of state power companies saying he would "take appropriate action against those utilities and their management if they do not meet their obligations to New Yorkers in this time of crisis."[58] One week after Hurricane Sandy, New Jersey Governor Chris Christie warned utilities they would face "Hurricane Chris" if electricity wasn't restored to everyone by the end of the week. This was after 2.2 million customers' power had been restored and

500,000 remained without power. He said restoration of 2 million customers "doesn't mean a damn to you if your power is not back."[59]

Thanks governors for the support of your utilities who throw everything they have at storm restoration. I'm sure you'll use the same standard to evaluate your road-clearing response to the next big blizzard. Surely the governor will be able to communicate accurately when my street will be cleared. The nature of politics is to armchair quarterback and scream for the firing of the coach no matter how hard the team played in a close loss.

The facts of the matter are that no system can provide infallible power at an affordable cost. As Phil Carson, former editor of the electric power industry website Energy Central, pointed out, "Utilities have no choice but to be honest about the fallibility of their systems simply because it's true. Customers and their elected representatives probably need to be more honest with themselves about this element of the bigger picture."[60]

My logical side agrees with Carson. But the reality of human nature leads me to believe a more balanced understanding of our system fallibilities is not going to happen. We are living in a world where customers want it all, and they want it now. And they are getting it all and getting it now from a number of companies that are giving them overnight delivery and instant real-time critical information. So they are beginning to expect it from their utility too. More education will not put a dent in public understanding. Redesign of our outage restoration communication processes and systems is what is required.

As I stated earlier, utilities will be doomed to the fate of the legacy airlines if they do not apply new technologies and redesign processes so they can provide specific restoration times to each customer. Airlines do a tremendous job, at a relatively low price point, in safely transporting people across huge distances in a short amount of time. Yet things break on airplanes that interrupt service. Just like utilities. And "acts of God" throw airlines curves that cause great consumer inconvenience. Just like utilities. And airlines throw everything they've got at getting things back on track. Just like utilities. Yet airline passengers are mad because of the inconvenience and the inability of airlines to give them accurate and timely information. Just like utilities.

Interestingly, one of the selling points for smart grid often quoted by utility leaders was that customers would no longer need to call to report an outage. I think customers would happily trade the benefit of not reporting an outage for receiving a timely and accurate estimated time of restoration (ETR). Customers today have relative ease in reporting outages because of high-capacity automated phone systems and online/mobile reporting tools. What they really want is having their power restored, and in the meantime, receiving timely and accurate information on the status of their individual restoration.

It is critical that utilities have a C-level strategic commitment to improve their outage communication processes. Senior levels need to have a clear view of the existing process, its gaps and opportunities, and a plan for moving forward. They need to understand there is no escaping the escalating consumer and regulatory requirements for increased communication. They also need to understand that this increased communication exposes that your data is not as precise as it needs to be to accurately communicate with your customers. You must have a long-term commitment, urgency to act, and C-level commitment to build the culture, processes, and technology required to communicate specific outage and restoration information to Me, Myself & I.

This journey has a system piece and a cultural piece that are critical to your plan. One is how you tie together Distribution Management Systems (DMS), Outage Management Systems (OMS), Customer Information Systems (CIS), and Customer Contact infrastructure together. This will be discussed in more detail in Chapter 17, "A New Taxonomy."

The second is possibly the biggest hurdle. There is a significant cultural challenge of getting operations employees to internalize the importance of providing outage assessment and restoration times. Understandably, the typical operations employee is focused on doing everything they can to restore power as quickly as possible. Taking time to report outage cause, damage assessment, and estimated time of restoration is seen as taking away from their Job One—restoring power as soon as possible. But it is clear the customer is demanding not just quick restoration but also communication. Utilities need to establish a change management action plan that results in operations understanding the importance for providing restoration information on an equally high pedestal with restoring service.

The bottom line is that customers generally are not going to give you credit for improvements in reliability because it is something that is difficult for them to perceive. What they can readily see and feel is an outage. And their expectation of how you respond to their outage reporting and inquiries is going through the roof.

Redesign your outage reporting, restoration, and communications processes. . .or "welcome to the airline business!"

CHAPTER 9

Meter-to-Me

IT'S ABOUT ME

Typically, utility customer service has involved set a meter, bill a meter, and collect on the meter. Thus, the noncustomer-centric term, meter-to-cash, often used to describe utility customer care processes. To engage today's Me, Myself & I consumer, you must make them the focus of your customer service processes. Therefore, utility customer service must be meter-to-me.

METER-TO-ME REQUIRES A SMART METER

The one central change that is necessary for effective meter-to-me processes is a smart meter. How can you meet the needs of today's customers without a meter that has two-way digital communication that provides customers daily usage information, has the ability to provide pricing options, and can be remotely connected or disconnected?

How can we expect satisfied customers when we keep them in the dark on their consumption? How can we expect people to be efficient consumers of energy and good stewards of the environment when we hide their consumption from them? You can't help those with limited incomes get through their constant struggle to provide life's necessities when you provide a monthly bill weeks after the energy is consumed.

Customers are smart, always connected, always on, so how can we meet their expectations when we are isolated from the meter? You can't! Period! End of story! And if we don't, in our rapidly advancing technological society, others will bridge the gap and insert themselves between you and your customers. We can't continue to deliver outdated meter-to-cash processes built on a 100-year-old metering model.

The following examples illustrate how advanced metering enables the key meter-to-me offerings customers require in our connected world.

FROM MYSTERY TO CONTEXT

A unique characteristic of our industry is not enabling its customers to know their usage, and therefore their cost, until long after the purchase is complete. In other words, utilities provide their customers with monthly mystery bills.

Can you imagine the level of satisfaction you would have with your credit card company if they sent you a bill with only the total amount on it? Every month when I get my American Express bill, I look at the total and then immediately scream, "This can't be right!" Then I look at the detail, show it to my wife and daughters—and I'll be damned, it's right every time. Why would we expect our customers to look at a utility bill and think it is right when we are only showing them the total for the month?

There has been considerable discussion about utilities needing to become their customers' trusted energy advisor. If you want to be trusted, you better be able to have your customers believe their bill. Believability starts with the ability to have at least daily usage information.

It is also critical to provide context. If you ask people what a gallon of gasoline costs, they can tell you with a high degree of accuracy. They know generally what it costs to fill their tank and how long it will last them. Consumers have no similar context for their electric bill. They may know their average monthly bill but have little understanding beyond that. We need to begin to build a utility bill context for customers that they can understand.

My Nest thermostat, with a couple of swipes of the finger, shows me the number of hours my heating or cooling runs each day and the time of day it ran. It also shows whether the change from the previous day was driven by weather or by my thermostat settings. Nest is providing me a relevant and understandable context for the biggest driver of the consumption and variability in my energy bill.

Energy reports can provide customers the context of how their usage compares against efficient neighbors and all neighbors. Sacramento, California's, municipal utility, SMUD, found that 30 months after the first quarterly energy usage reports were sent that there was an average of 2.6 percent electricity savings for high-consumption households and 1.5 percent savings for lower-consumption households.[61] By providing consumers an "mpg" context on where they stand compared to others, SMUD has had an impact on reducing consumption.

Before the recent federal stimulus fueled deployment of smart meters, customers on prepay plans were the few who could have some idea of what they were using daily and its cost. The value of this information is demonstrated by the fact that prepay customers have the information that enables them to take control of their energy consumption. Energy management consulting firm DEFG studied Oklahoma Electric Cooperative's prepaid customers and found that they reduced their energy bills by 11 percent. DEFG's CEO, Jamie Wimberly, stated, "This study supports the notion that regular communication providing timely data where usage is tied to dollars and cents is key to a shift in energy consumption."[62]

With smart meters, utilities can provide even greater consumption context and awareness by providing their customers online energy tools that combine daily usage with weather data and household information. Arizona's Salt River Project (SRP) customers can see on the web their daily usage compared to daily temperature. Additionally, customers can compare their bills to similarly sized and equipped homes. Consumers have a thirst for this information demonstrated by the fact that SRP's most visited web page is the one with daily usage information. SRP is killing the monthly mystery bill.[63]

FROM HELPLESSNESS TO CHOICES AND CONTROL

The most common source of complaint is "the bill." The monthly mystery bill aspects discussed earlier drive a major portion of these complaints. But a corresponding large portion of bill complaints is driven by the lack of choices and, therefore, the perception of the lack of control over their energy bill.

Since the Carter Administration, we have been educating customers on energy efficiency and reducing their bills. During my career, spanning four decades, I repeatedly told customers in the winter to turn down their thermostat and put on a sweater. I've got to believe many of those customers are beginning to look like Ralphie's younger brother, Randy, in the holiday movie classic *Christmas Story*, whose mom had wrapped him in so many layers of winter clothing that he could barely move.

We fail to realize that the majority of our customers have listened to us and have done many of the things we've asked them to do. The 2014 *Deloitte reSources Study* reported consumers are already doing the basics to lower electricity bills, with 85 percent of consumers saying they turn off the lights when they leave the room, and 71 percent saying they shut off electronics when not in use. Additionally, Deloitte reported two-thirds (68 percent) of households say they are doing all they can to keep their electric bills down.[64]

The mental state of utility customers was poetically stated in a letter to the editor titled "Ode to My Utility." Unfortunately, I lost the web link and cannot properly cite the source. Fortunately, though, I wrote down the poem.

Ode to My Utility

As I wonder and wait each day,
What will I find in the silver box at the end of my driveway?

As I open the door so carefully,
What do I see,
A utility bill waving at me.

On the top next to my name are the words, "Save Energy—Save Money."

I just knew since it was past Christmas, they had me in mind,
When they stamped "Save Energy—Save Money" beside my name.

Because, you see,
I didn't burn the Christmas lights that were all over my yard,
Because they would use too much energy.

I had to keep reminding the kids to turn off the energy-efficient TV,
Because they would use too much energy.

We hauled in wood and made a fire so the heat pump would not use so much energy.

I used the air-dry method for drying clothes because the electric dryer would use too much energy.

I cooked lots of things in the oven at one time so we would not use so much energy.

I practice all these energy-saving tips each month.

So, to my surprise, after saving all that energy, my bill was $110 more than the previous month.

Now I understand how to save energy.

So would someone please help me understand how to "Save Money"?

Customers want to reduce their bills and save money. But for the most part, our customers have done most of the easy low-hanging-fruit energy reducers. What's left involves large long-term capital investments or major changes in lifestyle, comfort, and convenience. Thus customers believe they have hit the wall for energy savings. And to a large extent they have because of our industry's extremely limited offerings. When you only offer one or two rate options tied to a monthly mystery billing process it is difficult for a customer to find ways to reduce their bill that fits with their lifestyle, comfort, and convenience preferences.

Much has recently been written about the need to design offerings to specific market segments of customers in order to more effectively engage them with energy programs, products, and services. Much of the stated benefits have been oriented toward customer engagement. But we are missing the more powerful benefit—moving customers from a feeling of helplessness to one of control.

Energy economists Dr. Karl McDemott and Dr. Carl R. Peterson make the point in their National Economic Research Associates (NERA) white paper, *Innovation in Retail Electricity Markets: The Overlooked Benefit*, that customer happiness is about choice. And choice is not only about price, but convenience, quality, environmental attributes, and control over usage.[65]

That is what Oklahoma Gas & Electric (OG&E) is achieving with their product that allows customers to program their thermostat for either comfort or convenience. If you program for savings, it will automatically adjust your thermostat up during periods of high demand and save customers on average $175 to $200 annually. OG&E's chairman Peter Delaney reports, "We've seen customer satisfaction really skyrocket with these programs, because they're more in control and can make their own decisions."[66]

SRP also allows their customers to be more in control, which has resulted in SRP being ranked highest in the large utility segment in the West for the seventh consecutive year by J.D. Power and Associates' 2014 *Residential Electric Utility Customer Satisfaction* study. "The concept of customer choice is embedded in their culture and programs,"[67] reported an Association for Demand Response & Smart Grid case study. SRP has 31 percent of their residential customers on various pricing alternatives that vary by time of day, and 17 percent of their customers have selected prepay electric service.[68]

Jeff Conklin, senior director of J.D. Power's energy utility practice, states, "Creating awareness and motivating customers to engage with new energy programs, products, and services is a huge opportunity for utilities to improve customer satisfaction. Customer satisfaction is higher when consumers are merely aware of programs, and then satisfaction increases substantially with each additional program a consumer joins."[69]

SRP's customers live in some of the hottest temperatures on the planet. Most cannot live without their air conditioning and demand a degree of comfort. The ability to lower their bill by raising the thermostat, closing blinds, and insulating their home has been done long ago by the majority of them. What SRP has done so well is give their customers multiple options. SRP enables their customers to go from a feeling of helplessness to one of being in control.

"Only about a dozen utilities excel at offering a wide variety of options for their customers," says Conklin. "While many other utilities do a good job, far too many utilities lag behind in engaging their customers."[70]

We have spent a lot of effort telling customers what they can do on their side of the meter to save energy. It is now time for us to turn our attention to providing customers numerous pricing and demand response options.

FROM PAYMENTS TO CONVENIENCE

Utility payment strategy has historically been one of providing a level of access and convenience while maintaining a baseline cost level. Not too many years ago the majority of utility payments were sent through the mail or made at local offices. As technology centralized back-office work and customers looked to do more over the phone and Internet, many local customer service offices were replaced by third-party payment centers to provide an ability to make local payments.

I believe it will always be critical to provide local access to make cash payments. This is especially important for customers facing disconnection for nonpayment. I don't advocate that all payments will become cashless. But it is important to understand that the majority of utility customers have embraced the cashless lifestyle. Not just credit cards but now debit and prepaid cards. And as customers have become always connected, always on, their cards will be replaced by mobile apps and digital wallets. One only needs to look to Starbucks for evidence of this growing trend. In the fourth quarter of fiscal year 2014, 33 percent of Starbucks' U.S. retail revenue in company-owned stores was paid on a prepaid card or mobile app.[71] Apple's recent announcement of their ApplePay functionality, which makes it extremely simple and highly secure to pay by touching your phone to a payment terminal, will only accelerate this adoption of digital wallets.

A national consumer survey, completed by EcoAlign, a strategic marketing agency and DEFG, a management consulting firm specializing in energy, found that 55 percent of consumers had used or purchased a prepaid card or service and that 38 percent of Americans would be interested in prepaid electricity.[72]

Historically, utilities have focused on electronic payments through the customer's bank. Because of the desire to maintain the cost of payment alternatives to some baseline level, utilities generally do not offer no-fee credit card or debit card payments. If you want to pay by credit card, many utilities will connect you with a third-party service that will charge up to $6 to take your credit card payment. Hence, the most prevalent source of utility electronic payment has been electronic check payments debited to customers' checking or bank accounts.

Frankly, that is so 2000 and not how utility customers pay the majority of their other purchases. Focusing on web and electronic bank payments will only leave a utility further behind. More and more customers are leaving the web to pay their bills by adopting digital wallets because it is a natural extension of how they are living.[73]

If utilities in our digital world are to meet their customers' payment experience requirements, there are a number of hurdles they need to overcome. First, is eliminating payment fees.

However, with high-speed mail payment processing costing around a dime and electronic payments being as low as pennies, migrating customers to credit card fees of 1 to 2 percent on an average bill of $100 is a prohibitive cost increase for utilities to absorb.

Most retailers understand that offering credit and debit cards is a cost of doing business and necessary to keep up with their competitors. Therefore, they spread the costs across all purchases. Progressive utilities that want to adopt these cashless methods will find a major hit to their bottom line, at least until the next rate case, as they absorb these costs. Many regulators and consumer advocates do not want these costs allocated across all customers, but prefer to have the users bear the costs. Until utilities are able to timely pass along these costs, they will not enable their customers to pay their utility bills in the same manner they pay the majority of their bills. In a utility environment, this might be acceptable. But it will become increasingly unacceptable to customers in our digital world. It will also be a challenge for increasing customer engagement with online and mobile programs where customers expect to pay for free using credit, debit or digital wallets like they do everywhere else.

Another obstacle is legacy systems' ability to keep up with customers' payment experience requirements. For example, standing in line at Starbucks I can look at my iPhone app and see that I don't have enough money on my prepaid card to buy a cup of coffee. With a couple touches, I can add money to my card by charging my credit card. *Voila*—my card is immediately updated. I reach the counter and place my order. I purchase my coffee by holding my phone up to a scanner. I walk away with my coffee, and my balance is immediately updated. Customers live in a real-time world where their transactions are immediately reflected. Compare this to many utility legacy systems where it may take a day to reflect a payment. Utilities must at least build a common payment interface in front of their legacy systems so that they can reflect payment transactions in real-time.

The final obstacle is the monthly bill. I've heard DEFG CEO Jamie Wimberly state that we need to "blow up the monthly bill." He's not saying we need to eliminate the monthly bill but that we need to understand that customers want to pay in many different ways on many different terms. This means it won't always be a monthly bill.

I couldn't agree more. We must offer customers numerous options on how they pay their bill and how often. We need to realize that technology and retail are making prepaid and daily or weekly billing a lifestyle and convenience choice. We must build billing and payment capabilities that match our customers' lifestyle preferences.

FROM APPOINTMENTS TO ON-DEMAND

We are in an on-demand world. FedEx has conditioned us to expect everything and anything "absolutely, positively overnight." The entertainment industry is being disrupted because consumers demand content on their schedule. DirecTV On-Demand, HBO Go, Apple TV, and Netflix are all about delivering content on their customers' terms.

Amazon Prime provides free shipping with two-day delivery on all purchases. Want it faster, and there is an option to buy overnight delivery. Most online retailers understand that they must provide options to the growing segment of customers who want it all and want it now.

Being isolated from the meter, from an information and control standpoint, always meant that utilities generally had to roll a truck and have a technician physically access the meter to complete a customer service request. In many locations, this required an appointment because the meter was inside or inaccessible due to locked fences and unfriendly dogs. This meant that the customer's request could only be met on weekdays during normal work hours. And if an appointment was required, usually the best we could do was to provide a four-hour window.

There were countless times I was unable to deliver a good customer experience because of what was required to access a meter. The most frustrating of all was receiving the call from a customer who had been disconnected for nonpayment on a Friday morning, only to come home that evening and find they were without electricity. Often this was a single parent with young children who faced being without electricity the entire weekend because we didn't do reconnects on weekends. Or if we did, it was accompanied with a significant reconnect fee the customer couldn't afford. It is wonderful having a smart electric meter where you can timely reconnect a customer after they have made a payment or turn on a new customer's service any day they want. In today's digitally connected world that is the way it should be.

We are in an on-demand world where consumers want it all and want it now. This means it is time for utilities and regulators to support installation of electric meters with remote connect/disconnect functionality.

FROM BORING TO ENGAGING

The Smart Grid Consumer Collaborative report, *Voices of Experience: Insights on Smart Grid Customer Engagement*, states, "The success of the smart grid will depend in part on consumers taking a more proactive role in managing their energy use."[74] I couldn't agree more, but consumers taking a larger proactive role will depend more on the utility than the consumer. It will depend on utilities delivering experiences in ways that interest customers and are happening where and how a customer lives. It will demand utilities deliver products, services, and experiences that are exciting. Even fun!

I believe gamification has a huge potential for solving utilities' customer engagement challenge. The Engagement Alliance is an organization to further research education and collaboration in gamification and engagement science. The Alliance defines gamification as the process of using game mechanics and game thinking in nongaming contexts to engage users and to solve problems. Gamification leverages game design, loyalty program design, and behavioral economics to create the optimal context for behavior change and successful outcomes.[75]

Components of gamification have been around for decades. Those my age will remember S&H Green Stamps. Consumers would receive paper green stamps for their gasoline, supermarket, and retail purchases. These stamps could be accumulated and then traded for merchandise selected from an S&H catalog. I remember numerous merchants also having punch cards. For each cup of coffee or sandwich your card would be punched, and when you had 10 purchases, you would get the next one free. Many will remember hounding their parents to buy more cereal to collect enough box tops to send away for the superhero decoder ring or the baking powder submarine. Cracker Jack built their whole brand on "a prize in every box."

Digital computing, connectivity, and graphical user interfaces have brought gamification to a new level by making the interaction with the customer easy, immediate, and more compelling. Interactive online design enables companies to use customers' competitive instincts to drive action through the use of virtual rewards, such as points, badges, payments, free gifts, discounts, and status indicators, such as retweets, leaderboards, progress bars, and achievement data.[76] More important connectivity allows companies to interact with their customers across the device and channel of their choice. "Big data" allows companies to tailor the offering, message and game design to the individual customer to achieve even bigger results.

To many, it seems irrational that consumers would be more engaged if they had a remote chance to win a small prize, or could compete to earn a badge, or engaged repeatedly just so they could see their name on a leaderboard. The reality is that to engage consumers with energy, we must go beyond the logic of price, environment, and efficiency. Why? Gabe Zicherman, chair of the GSummit where top gamification experts across industries gather to share knowledge and insight about employee and customer engagement and loyalty, says generally everyone knows what they need to do to lower their energy bill, be more efficient and protect the environment: Turn off the lights, turn down your thermostat, and buy efficient appliances. It's just like losing weight—people know they need to eat less and exercise more. Even though they understand it, they don't do it. Zicherman, says we must speak to customers' emotional core.[77]

Speaking to customers' emotional core is brought home in the following programs:

- San Diego Gas & Electric (SDG&E) used gamification in its 2012 initiative called the San Diego Energy Challenge. It invited customers who were within the San Diego Unified School District to compete on behalf of their middle school. Customers had a chance to not only earn individual prizes but enable their school to win a cash grant based on how much energy they saved on Reduce Your Use Days. SDG&E awarded $26,500 to eight middle schools.[78]

- Delmarva Power piloted the Delmarva Energy Challenge with 56,000 residential customers in Wilmington, Delaware. Customers were provided a fun way to monitor their energy usage, learn about ways to save, and compete with their friends and neighbors to save energy and win prizes not only for themselves but also their favorite Wilmington K-12 public school.[79]

I understand clearly why the SDG&E and Delmarva used social gamification techniques in their program design. A utility offering me $10 to $20 each summer month for a demand response program will not get my attention. Quite frankly, I don't think $50 a month would work. But when my granddaughter asks me to participate in an energy reduction contest for their school, I will be shedding significant load.

We must quit being so rational in the design of our products and services. We must learn to make energy appealing, fun, and engaging.

CHAPTER 10

MySelf Service

THE JOURNEY TO DO-IT-YOURSELF

The AT&T divestiture in the late '80s and the FCC order in 1992 for phone number portability ushered in the growth of toll-free phone numbers as a customer service channel.[80] Many companies proudly branded their products with the ability for consumers to call them toll-free to have their questions answered or problems solved by a customer service representative (CSR). This new access meant customers could easily contact companies with their questions or problems. This led to an increase in the number of customer calls, which led to the development of call centers, which resulted in increased customer service costs.

Enter Interactive Voice Response (IVR) technology, which enabled customers to receive updates on their account status, such as balance and last payment. These IVRs created opportunities for companies to reduce costs by decreasing the number of CSR-assisted contacts. As IVRs demonstrated their efficiency and effectiveness for basic account inquiry, companies expanded the types of interactions that could be completed. With the advance of speech recognition IVR technology, even more complex self-service transactions could be offered.

As the Internet grew, HTML enabled companies to offer a visual medium to self-service. This enabled even more complex transactions and support to take place over the Internet. Consequently, a larger percentage of customer interaction is occurring through self-service IVR and the web. Marsh reports that by 2020, 85 percent of interactions will occur without the customer interacting with a human being.[81]

In fact, the success of the well-designed self-service customer experience is making a myth out of "people just want to talk to a representative." The majority of customers now try to solve their question or problem themselves before attempting to call a CSR.[82] A recent survey by IntelliResponse, a virtual agent software company, indicated two-thirds of customers go straight to a company's website when they need answers[83] and half the smartphone users prefer self-service on their device.[84] Accenture's *Actionable Insights for the New Energy Consumer* study reported that utility consumers are making a dramatic move toward low-touch channels such as email or web. Even the more complex issues, such as switching to a new electricity provider, signing up for new services, and resolving billing issues, are seeing in the range of 40 percent of customers desiring self-service.[85]

However, a couple of interesting trends are developing. First, there are a large number of companies with IVRs and websites that have not seen a corresponding decrease in representative-assisted calls. Ease of access through the IVR and web has made getting simple answers more convenient and, therefore, has increased the number of times the customers inquire through these self-service channels. But it has not reduced the number of representative-assisted calls because these complex inquiries require more capable self-service architectures and systems. Much of the increase in the percentage of self-service calls is not because they've replaced agent-assisted calls but because the pie is getting bigger since customers are contacting utilities more.

Second, some are starting to see a downward trend in the percentage of contacts successfully handled through self-service. As customers have grown more web savvy, their expectations of what they want to accomplish through the web has significantly increased. Consumers now go to websites expecting to accomplish much more than they used to. But many web self-service capabilities have not kept up with the level of complexity in their customers' inquiries. This is demonstrated by a recent study from the Technology Services Industry Association (TSIA), which reports the percentage of customers who successfully resolve their self-service inquiry has fallen from 48 percent in 2003 to 39 percent in 2011.[86] This is an incredible statistic when you consider the dramatic improvement in companies' web capabilities over the last decade. It clearly points to the fact that consumers' expectations for their self-service experience has outpaced the substantial improvements companies have made in their offerings.

Ubiquitous digital connectivity has increased the opportunity for consumers to successfully serve themselves. The devices, connections, and capabilities are dramatically changing. Self-service is radically moving beyond IVR and the web. Yet rushing to add more channels will not necessarily wow customers, especially as their expectations rise for the level of complexity they wish to accomplish themselves.

In its study, *The Current State of Unassisted Support*, TSIA reported:

> Though companies frequently complain that they struggle to increase customer adoption of self-service, these numbers tend to indicate that customer adoption is not the problem. If 100

percent of customers who attempted self-service were success-ful, the percentage of issues resolved by self-service would easily grow to nearly one-half of all interactions. The challenge is not to convince more customers to try self-service; the real chal-lenge is to answer their questions once they are there, instead of sending 71 percent of self-service contacts to another channel to support.[87]

The truth is, much of self-service has been about reduc-ing call center costs, not about engagement, loyalty, and sat-isfaction. Some companies have a cram-and-contain strategy when it comes to their IVRs. We have spent tons of money on IVRs, but the fact is that most people dislike them. To funda-mentally affect representative-assisted call volume and meet today's always-connected, always-on customers' self-service expectations, you must significantly change how you design and deliver self-service.

THE MYSELF SERVICE REQUIREMENT

We must change our orientation from self-service to MySelf Service. The difference between the two is enormous.

The best example of self-service is when you go to a fast-food restaurant, eat your meal, and then clean your own table. How we've allowed ourselves to be conditioned to bus our own tables is beyond my comprehension. But we do. And that is self-service at its worst—doing something for the cor-poration that has little-to-no benefit to the customer.

Usually the primary focus of self-service is cost reduction, so often the customer becomes a low priority. For example, many companies focus on a measure called containment—the percentage of customers you're able to keep in the IVR rather than opting out or escalating to a CSR. Containment is always good for nuclear power, prisoners, hazardous waste, and baby diapers. It is not always good for the customer experience. If your priority is keeping the customer in the IVR, then it is not a good thing if it is at the expense of conveniently solving the customer's need.

MySelf Service, on the other hand, has just as much, if not more, benefit to the customer than to the corporation. The best example is airline check-in where 68 percent of passengers use the self-service.[88] There is a benefit to the airlines in terms of reduced processing costs, but the benefit to the customer is huge because they can choose a way to check in that is convenient and fits their lifestyle. Waiting in lines is nil, and I fulfill my need on my timetable. MySelf Service is intentionally designed to my benefit as much as the corporation's.

MySelf Service makes life easier. It's that simple. If what you are offering on the IVR, web, mobile, or app isn't clearly making life easier for your customers, then you have self-service. Even though surveys are beginning to report customers preferring to try self-service first, what they are really looking for is easy and simple. Customers today will take the path of least resistance.

The focus of self-service on lowering costs by driving more customer contact to self-service resolution has historically been effective because consumers generally had to accept being in the IVR jail of endless menu options, offering everything except what I need to solve my problem. However, the power today is in the consumers' hands. They clearly know when service is designed with them in mind or just a ruse to cut costs. If your self-service doesn't easily and conveniently resolve their need, they will call you. And when that doesn't work, they will take their case to social media.

MySelf Service requires that technology-assisted processes require less effort from the customer. We need to remember that our customers are investing their own time in our customer service processes. Therefore, we should reward their investment by enabling them to resolve their need themselves, with a minimal amount of effort—free of hoops, hurdles, roadblocks, and BS.[89]

Today's Me, Myself & I customers demand that service be designed specifically for them. These powerful consumers are not to be contained where they don't want to be. Consumers demand that your channels be designed primarily for their needs, not the corporation's, so we must orient our channels to provide MySelf Service.

START WITH IVR AND WEB

Just running out to add more channels to your existing self-service channels won't be enough because all self-service with today's powerful consumer must be first and foremost about Me, Myself & I. It is important your first response to the digital impact be building a culture that focuses on delivering self-service processes that are built with the customer in mind. That is, first focus on delivering MySelf Service through your existing channels. It is fine to add some basic mobile and app functionality if you feel you must hurry up and have a presence on the new digital channels. But replicating old self-service to more channels will not result in engaged customers. It is critical to start with your existing IVR and web services because they are likely your most used self-service channels today. By designing your existing channels with the customer in mind, you have a foundation of proper MySelf Service design orientation to apply to the other channels as you begin to offer them to customers.

MONITORING SOCIAL. . .WHILE ROME BURNS!

A high degree of attention and a large amount of resources have been paid to monitoring social media. Many companies have learned the hard way that they must constantly monitor social media for customer experience failures and intervene to resolve them before they go viral and do considerable brand damage.

High-performance call centers dedicate resources to actively monitor agent-assisted calls in order to tailor individual coaching and training for performance improvement. They also regularly measure first-contact resolution to identify areas of service failure and need for improvement.

My complaint is as self-service has become a majority of customer interactions, we have not seen a corresponding increase in the resources to monitor self-service channels in order to understand the failures that are occurring there. According to a Unisphere Research study, *Power to the People: Online Self-Service Evolves,* the average successful resolution rates for online self-service channels are:[90]

- *Telephone (IVR):* 61 percent
- *Website:*   48 percent
- *Mobile web/apps:* 29 percent

When it comes to monitoring social media, we are, in effect, monitoring the experiences of the powerful minority and ignoring the experiences of the majority. We must be sure that as we focus on monitoring social, Rome isn't burning. It's important we dedicate resources to monitor all customer experience channels in order to identify the pain points we're creating for our customers.

RESOLVE PAIN POINTS

MySelf Service requires that you start with the customer in mind. A good place for utilities to start is with the customer's pain points. Utilities receive millions of calls a year. These customers are calling, not to thank their utilities for reliable, affordable, convenient service, but because of a pain point: monthly mystery bill, payment posting, billing accuracy, establishing service, appointments, third-party agencies, deposits, and on and on. MySelf Service starts with making things painless, simple, and convenient for your customers.

The next requirement of MySelf Service is that it works flawlessly. First-contact resolution is a common call center quality metric. A 70 to 80 percent first-contact resolution is considered an excellent performance level for many call centers because it is recognized that many of the inquiries are complex and will not be resolved at the time of the call. But with self-service, the customer expects it to work. If it doesn't work, they are not only dissatisfied, but they are unlikely to want to use that channel again. Therefore, the functions you apply self-service to must work every time. And when they don't, you must provide a quick path to a representative.

If you don't have an easy way for your customers to reach a CSR, then you are putting them through hell to reach you, which is especially bad for those who routinely try to serve themselves first. For example, a large percentage of your customers are likely going to the web first. When they are unable to resolve their need, in the absence of click-to-chat or other easily found escalation path, they are likely to pick up the phone and call your 800 number . . . only to find themselves in a complex IVR menu that forces them to pick a menu path to resolve their problem. But the fact is, if your online web services were not able to resolve the customer's inquiry, then it is very unlikely that your IVR will be of any help. And now you have taken the best customers you have, those who want to serve themselves, and contained them in IVR menu hell. This is no way to treat your customers.

We are in a time where customers have many choices on how they want to interact with your company. So trust that the majority of them will make the best choice. Most of them today don't want to have lengthy conversations with your CSRs. They're busy with their lives and want to move on. So make it easy for them to get their answer. And when they can't, make it easy for them to get to a representative.

RIGHT-SIZE YOUR CHANNELS

Each channel has its own set of unique qualities that create their own set of advantages and disadvantages that must be matched against your customers' needs, wants, and lifestyles. MySelf Service requires that you right-size your channels to the business processes you are automating and to how your customers want to experience your service.

It's critical in your MySelf Service orientation to understand that all channels are not created equal and that you must resist the temptation to treat them the same by trying to force the same processes across all of them. Conventional wisdom is that customers would rather talk to a representative. However, I believe it is the excess application of certain self-service channel technologies that has created this misperception. We need to understand that every channel is not meant to be a great customer experience for every type of interaction and for every customer. We must right-size each channel to what it is best designed for.

A recent Cisco study says 52 percent of shoppers prefer self-checkout stations to avoid waiting in lines. That means the other half of shoppers don't.[91] Does that mean self-checkout is a bad channel? Absolutely not. It means it works great for certain situations and not well for others. For example, grocery self-checkout works great if you have few items and not a lot of fruits and vegetables. If I shop for a large family and fill my cart, the last thing I would like is self-checkout. It's a great idea for grocery stores to offer both self-checkout and full-service checkout, and to allow the customers to choose which aisle they want to use. It would be a very stupid idea for them to understaff the checkout clerks in an attempt to force the majority of their customers through the self-serve checkout. It would be insanely stupid to make only the self-checkout aisles visible to the customers by hiding the path to the full-service aisles.

Take my grocery store example and compare it to your self-service strategy. What thinking are you using for the path into and through your service channels?

MySelf Service focuses on building applications and services that are tightly designed to a group of customers whose lifestyle and preferences fit that specific channel. It's not about getting the majority of people crammed and contained through it.

THE IVR IS DEAD. . .LONG LIVE THE IVR

IVRs have a bad reputation—much of it deserved. Contact Solutions, a self-service solutions provider, reported in their *2013 Consumer Attitudes Towards Self-Service* study that only 18.2 percent of IVR users have been satisfied or extremely satisfied after using an automated voice menu. The study further found that 79.9 percent would rather wait on hold five minutes for a real person than use an IVR.[92]

IVRs are a great service tool for reoccurring and simple inquiries and transactions. They have become an even greater service channel as phones have become mobile and are now with one at all times. But we need to acknowledge that IVRs, like all self-service platforms, need to be right-sized to fit their unique characteristics. In fact, I will be so bold as to proclaim, "The IVR is dead…long live the IVR."

Traditional IVRs play an important role in self-service. But we need to quit trying to cram and contain more and more into them. Since we're very poor listeners, complexity in an IVR means customers will get lost and frustrated. The focus needs to be on identifying the inquiries and interactions best suited for the IVR, and continuous monitoring and evaluation of the IVR paths to ensure that a high degree of resolution and satisfaction is happening within them. And for heaven's sake, make the path to a CSR obvious and easy.

That is why I say the "IVR is dead." Traditional IVR contacts are important but will not be a growing percentage of self-service contacts because consumers are increasingly becoming connected to smartphones, phablets, and tablets, which provide a visual medium to the self-service process. As a result, consumers will naturally migrate to the visual channels and away from the IVR for the majority of their service interactions.

The IVR may be dead, but there is new technology evolving that will give the IVR new life—"Long Live the IVR." Think Siri and others of her kind: The virtual assistant or digital concierge means we're entering a time when self-service becomes conversational.

VIRTUAL ASSISTANTS

Virtual agents are software services that enable automated conversations with customers in self-service environments. Virtual agents serve as round-the-clock research agents that sit on digital channels to collect customer questions and task-related queries.[93] Collecting these questions at scale in the hundreds of thousands enables companies in real-time to understand the themes and trends around their self-service interactions. This information enables companies to make sure they can direct their customers to the right place to solve their inquiry or demonstrates where they need to enhance their self-service offerings.

Again the customer is demanding, "make my life easier." Finding the answer on a website or a small mobile screen can be just as daunting as it is in an IVR menu. Making escalation available makes life easier. But escalation to a representative is expensive. Virtual agents makes customers' lives easier by escalating their inquiry to intelligence within the self-service channel and enabling them to quickly get the information to resolve their inquiry.

These IVR or web virtual agents use artificial intelligence built from experience, using a combination of natural language and knowledge bases to handle complex conversations.[94] The key here is building intelligence from the conversations service agents or virtual agents have every day.

The software intelligence enabling virtual assistants provides an opportunity for self-service to become conversational. As virtual agents and speech recognition evolves, a large number of customers will be happy to talk to your Siri.

CHAPTER 11

Fingertip Resolution

LET YOUR FINGERS DO THE WALKING

It used to be that the best you could do with your fingertips to resolve an issue was to "let your fingers do your walking through the Yellow Pages." For you nonancient readers, this was a popular advertising slogan for the Yellow Pages. In the days of yore, it was the easiest way to find the phone number for someone to contact in hopes of finding a solution to your need. It's hell to get old and have to explain your references.

LET YOUR FINGERS DO THE RESOLVING

Today's digital connectivity provides a huge opportunity for companies to serve content to their customers anywhere, at any time. As a result, customers today can resolve issues by letting their fingertips walk across a touch screen.

Unfortunately, many companies' focus has been on pushing to mobile platforms the same volumes of content and functionality contained on their web pages. However, businesses need to "think small" when it comes to mobile. Not just because the screen sizes are small, but also because customers today are in a hurry and usually interacting in small bites.[95]

It's also more than just pushing small bite-sized web content to another device. In his book *The Third Screen*, Chuck Martin states, "The relationship of the consumer to the device is not the passive 'lean back' of TV or the more active 'lean forward' of the PC but rather the fully interactive 'pull it forward' of mobile. It's up close, it's personal, and it's always on."[96]

Mobility creates accessibility that has not been there with any other technology. Always connected, always on means technology is always with us. Companies now have the opportunity to provide constant and intimate accessibility to their products and services. This presents a new and unique customer service opportunity to put at your customers' fingertips: specific, quick, easy, and relevant solutions to their recurring needs and wants.

For example, it used to be that when I heard of a TV program I wanted to record, I had to be home in front of my DVR. Or I had to call home in hopes of finding someone willing to do ol' Dad a favor and program his DVR. With my DirecTV, I now have an iPhone app that allows me access to their product at any time, from anywhere, and set any or all five DVRs in my home.

My Nest thermostat also has an iPhone app that allows me to adjust my household temperature from anywhere, at any time. When I go to bed, if the upstairs temperature is not comfortable, I do not need to go downstairs to adjust the thermostat. With Nest, I can adjust my thermostat from bed and sleep comfortably. When I'm traveling and set my thermostat back, I can conveniently reset the temperature as I near home so that it's comfortable when I walk in the door.

Delta Air Lines provides an app, that in just a few touches, allows me to look at my booked flights, check-in, check flight status, and track my bags. Hilton hotels is releasing an app that not only allows you to check-in and choose your room location in a couple of touches but also turns your smartphone into your room key.

"Fingertip" channel interactions enable customers to resolve their need immediately. With consumers living busy, cluttered, hectic, chaotic lives, they do not have the patience or tolerance for complication. They place a high value on convenience and simplicity. The Staples office supply chain understands this completely and has built their entire brand around the Easy Button. Mobility's intimacy and immediacy provides the ability for any company to place their version of the Easy Button at every smartphone owner's fingertips.

Trips to a store to talk to a representative, phone calls to a call center to resolve a need, online websites to search for the right page, take too much time. Give your customers the convenience and ease to accomplish their task on a touch screen, with just a couple swipes, and you've given them "fingertip resolution."

YOU HAD ME AT SWIPE, AND LOST ME AT TYPE AND SCROLL

Customers are looking for companies that can simplify their lives, make things convenient, and give them an Easy Button. Too often companies are behaving as if mobile is just another platform for delivering reams of web content. From the customer's viewpoint, nothing is more frustrating than trying to interface with a miniature touch screen when the design in front of them is rooted in the world of large-screen PCs.

The size, immediacy, and intimacy of mobile make it a channel that has the potential to create consumers who fall in love with your app. But it comes with very different user experience requirements. To conduct an excellent customer experience through a "fingertip" contact channel, its key attributes must be:

- *Frequently needed:* a need the customer has on a reoccurring basis
- *Accessible:* has a low barrier to entry; keeps me logged in rather than fumbling through user ID and password
- *Easy:* one or two swipes maximum, with minimum keyboard strokes
- *Immediate:* whatever I initiate is completed in real-time
- *Flawless:* works every time; confirms that it worked or alerts you when it didn't

The intimacy and immediacy of mobile presents a whole new level of performance metrics for an exceptional customer experience. Typical call center metrics get turned upside down: Average speed of answer becomes immediate. Average handle time becomes two to three swipes of the finger. And the most challenging—first-contact resolution—becomes that it works every time.

CASUAL VERTICAL ENGAGEMENT

Next time you're in a public place, look around. You will see a large number of people staring at their small screens. Whether standing in line at the bank, at the fast-food restaurant, or at airport security, consumers are frequently looking at their digital devices. According to a 2013 Nokia study, people can't leave their smartphone alone for more than six minutes and check them up to 150 times a day.[97] In other words, customers are conducting "casual vertical engagement."

Smart devices enable access to endless data, applications, and videos. This means consumers can fill their moments of inactivity with the digital screen. As this addiction to digital devices continues to grow, businesses have the opportunity to provide an app that customers choose as they scan their smart devices for something of interest to replace their moments of inactivity.

For example, from a personal perspective, while standing in line, I generally check my email, the Weather Channel, CNBC stock quotes, Facebook, and Twitter. Then I look at my Nest thermostat app to check my energy usage for the previous day. Next, I check my Starbucks card to see if my earlier purchase was applied to my loyalty status and how close I am to a free latte. Then I look at Redbox to see what movies are coming out this week that I might want to rent.

In my opinion, there is an opportunity here for utilities as they develop mobile strategies. If we build applications that take a lot of touches or have too much content, we are only going to engage customers when they have a deep need to inquire or look. But if in one or two touches a customer can look at yesterday's energy usage, then there is a chance utilities can be one of the applications customers look at daily as they fill their periods of inactivity with casual vertical engagement. Repeated interactions that customers value build real relationships.

UTILITY FINGERTIP RESOLUTION

The intimacy and immediacy of mobile presents an opportunity to reach out to your customer with information of value to them in a way that creates a conversation and a relationship. As utilities talk about the need to engage their customers, it is important to understand it doesn't mean being able to say, "We have an app for that." Mobile engagement means providing your customers convenience and simplicity. It's about enabling your customers to easily improve an area of importance in their lives.

J.D. Power reports the number of customers using their mobile device to access their utility website is increasing, yet they are having a less satisfying experience compared to accessing the site on their computer.[98] To me, that says we are focusing too heavily on porting the web to mobile or on having an app. Instead, we need to focus on where can we simplify and improve the customer's life.

For example, make it easy to eliminate the mystery in my bill. Provide an app that allows me to set a monthly budget and see if my usage is on course to be within my budget. Build this app so it is easy to access my daily usage information during my periods of casual vertical engagement. As your data analytics capabilities improve, provide me tailored energy-saving recommendations based on my specific usage, household, and weather.

Provide me a "Working for You" app that keeps me posted about the work in my area that improves reliability. The app would notify me of planned outages. It would alert me to pending bad weather and things I can do to prepare. It would allow me to preset quick outage reporting capabilities so when power is out, all I need to do is swipe my finger to report an outage—no fumbling in the dark to find my utility's phone number or my account number. It would then provide me with alerts updating me on my restoration.

It's not about rushing to build apps that replicate the web. It is about providing apps that make a customers' life simpler and easier in just a couple of swipes.

CHAPTER 12

In the Key of Me

SPEAK TO ME, NOT TO THE MASSES

It has been widely recognized that for smart energy to be successful, we must increase our communication. Historically, proactive communication for utilities meant blasting messages to the masses through bill stuffers and direct mail. Mobile connectivity means we can now broadcast these same messages through social media, like Twitter and Facebook. However, broadcasting mass messages will not be enough. Utilities must become more targeted in their communication efforts.

The Smart Grid Consumer Collaborative (SGCC) 2013 *State of the Consumer* report listed segmentation as a key theme. According the report, "Segmentation matters: Consumer values, desires, and motivations are not all the same." SGCC identified five distinct customer segments to tailor smart grid communications and programs to.[99] J.D. Power conducted a *Smart Grid Consumer Behavioral Segmentation* study that defined six behavioral segments based on the type of activities that diverse customer groups will take to manage their consumption, costs, and environmental impact. Their study identified considerable variation in types of strategies that should be undertaken to engage these diverse groups of customers.[100] Segmentation is a great start to more effective communication and engagement. But it is just a start.

In July 2012, at the Social Media Marketing Conference Summit in Amsterdam, Business Intelligence Group's chief analyst Peter Gentsch showed a slide listing the following demographic data:

- Born in 1948 and grew up in England
- Married twice
- Two children
- Successful in business
- Wealthy
- Winter holidays spent in the Alps
- Likes dogs

Gentsch then proceeded to point out two consumers who fit these demographics.[101]

Prince Charles   *Ozzy Osbourne*

Does that mean these two will respond in the same way to the same messages? It's unlikely.

Segmentation is an important marketing tool, but it is not a precise one. Social media is a powerful new communication channel, but much of the corporate messaging through this channel is to the masses. Today's consumer demands it be less about the masses and more about Me, Myself & I.

IBM's CEO, Ginni Rometty stated, "Big data will spell the death of customer segmentation and force the marketer to understand each customer as an individual within 18 months or risk being left in the dust." Rometty explains, "Marketers will say my job has always been to understand customer segments. The shift is to go from the segment to the individual. It spells the death of the average customer."[102]

Digital connectivity and big data mean you can tailor your communication and services to the individual. It used to be the best I could target was to the household via TV, radio, or outbound telemarketing. None of which assured I would reach the targeted individual. Mail may have reached the individual, but it lacked immediacy because it generally was opened at a later time of convenience—if it was opened at all. Email, too, is opened later, and often much later by today's millennials who check email last.

Today's digital connectivity means I can reach an individual customer through their device, which is with them at all times and all locations. Think keys, wallet, and smartphone.

Digital connectivity means I can reach the individual on a medium that has immediacy. Big data means I can reach them in an intelligent and value-creating way because I know each customer's preferences and habits, and build specific communication and interactions to them.

ME, MYSELF & I CONTROLS THE ENGAGEMENT

We discussed earlier that Me, Myself & I consumers are very powerful. They are in control of the messages and communications they pay attention to. Therefore, they are in control of which ones they respond to and thus the conversations and relationships they have. As a result, a huge challenge utilities face is being in a position to have the right conversations, in the right way, at the right time the consumer wants to have them.[103] The good news is that digital connectivity is allowing consumers to state their preferences for the conversations they want to have. It means you can provide your customers service "In the Key of Me.[SM]"

In the Key-of-Me service means:

- *Know Me:* Know who I am; know what has been communicated with me; know what service I need, know what is important for me to know; know what language I prefer.

- *Know My Communication:* Know how I like to be contacted: voice, email, SMS, web, social.

- *Know When to Contact Me*: Know how I like to be notified, when I like to be contacted, and under which contexts.[104]

THEY SHOOT TROJAN HORSES, DON'T THEY?

Unfortunately, customers are being bombarded with messages as new media platforms have proliferated. As the methods to communicate have increased, so has the level of junk messaging. In the Key of Me is not about getting the customer to click on a permission button that allows you to start barraging them with a bunch of marketing messages. I hate the number of permissions that are nothing more than a Trojan horse to get beyond the customer's wall so that you can inundate them with marketing messages. I am sick of the over 100 email messages I get each day because somewhere along the interaction path, I was tricked into opting in to a flood of email messages. What I love about the Apple iOS is that applications cannot do much of anything without a specific intervention that confirms that I do indeed want to allow them to access my location, use my microphone, and push alerts to me.

In the Key of Me is about being very specific about an offering to customers and delivering that offering as detailed by the customer. Avoid sneakiness and deception to get customer permission. The ever-increasing, powerful Me, Myself & I consumers do shoot Trojan horses, and customers inundated with a pile of unwanted messages will tune you out. Then any hope of having a critical message received, an action taken, or a product bought can be thrown out the window.

JUST GIVE ME OPTIONS, AND I WILL CHOOSE

Much of social media is a mass communication channel. Through segmentation, I can tailor messages to each segment, but you're using an imprecise science to target customers. What I propose is building applications you know a sizable number of your customers will value. Then ask them to subscribe and state their preference to receive that communication and engagement. Take advantage of their connectivity to tailor a specific message to a specific customer, on the subject and channel of their choosing, built on individual, specific, and valued contexts.

I believe utilities would be better served by allocating some of their market segmentation research budgets to provide preference management capabilities so their customers can tell them what they want. Because of the intimacy and immediacy of mobile connectivity and the capability of the back-office IT systems, you can now communicate with your customer on what they choose, when they choose, and in the method they choose. Build the applications and the preference management system that enables your customers to engage with you on their terms.

For example, Texas utility Oncor allows its customers to register from their phones and receive text alerts when their power is out, as well as updates on estimated time of restoration. It also allows customers to receive updates on selected service requests.[105] ComEd's *Outage Alert* program has nearly 730,000 customers signed up for their two-way texting service that notifies customers of an outage and provides updates on restoration.[106] Arizona's Salt River Project allows customers to set a monthly budget and receive text alerts regarding their progress toward meeting their goal.[107] Georgia Power allows its customers to state a preference on whether they want to receive outage alerts via text message, email, or automated phone call.[108]

These examples show there are a significant number of customers who want you to communicate with them. Allowing them to state their preferences gives you tremendous insight into each customer. This business intelligence obtained over time gives you the opportunity to communicate and interact with them individually and specifically on things they value.

It's providing service In the Key of Me.

CHAPTER 13

The New CSR—Customer Service Resolutionary

As utilities recognize the need to create stronger relationships with their customers, "trusted energy advisor" is becoming a common term. It implies that you provide additional resources to enable your customer service representatives (CSRs) to spend more time advising customers on how to manage their energy consumption.

But "trusted energy advisor" misses the change that is occurring with today's always-connected, always-on customers. While it recognizes that customers need much more information and control over their bill, it misses that fact that consumers today are already quite knowledgeable because they have access to the utility's information online, plus many other sources. In many cases, the customer has already received a lot of advice and is looking for something more. The Me, Myself & I consumer is looking for a resolution—now! E Source surveyed 1,000 residential customers on their expectations and found that 69 percent strongly agreed having their problem resolved immediately matters most.[109]

Rethinking customer service for our digital world means we must be viewed by our customers, not as an advisor, but as a "trusted energy *resolutionary*."[110] Our focus must be on empowering our employees with the tools and processes that enable them to rapidly deliver resolutions to customers' increasingly complex calls.

THE DEATH OF SIMPLE

It is wrong to believe that the importance of CSRs diminishes as self-service grows. The exact opposite is true. By its nature, self-service starts with easier calls. As your self-service capabilities grow, more difficult calls are completed. Over time, this increase in self-service leaves CSRs with only complex and challenging customer service calls. No longer can they get a break from the pressure of tough calls by receiving some easier ones, such as change of address, last payment received, or billing due date.

Additionally, those calls are likely to be from customers who are as smart, if not smarter, than your CSRs. By the time the customer contacts your call center, they have probably already Googled their problem, getting expert information and finding out what countless other consumers have experienced. More important, they know what processes, experiences, interactions, and channels they have been through with your company up to the point of your CSR answering the phone. How much will your CSR know when your smart customer calls?

MASS PRODUCTION VERSUS CUSTOMIZATION

Historically we've used scripts to train agents how to process calls with the goal of efficiently completing the call and creating a satisfied customer. This is the call center version of mass production.[111]

If the simple interactions are going away, and you are left with unique, diverse, complex, and difficult inquiries, then a mass production call center will not result in satisfied customers. Call center training and systems built for large volumes of homogeneous inquiries are not sufficient. Representatives trained to respond in rote are ill-equipped to be resolutionaries who must listen, think, investigate, and construct a solution to a unique inquiry.

It is critical that call centers have knowledge-based tools that enable representatives to easily access answers to the unique and complex inquiries. In fact, the same is needed for web and mobile inquiries. A key solution is using "virtual agents" to provide the intelligence needed to answer customers' inquiries. Virtual agents are software services that provide the ability to enter natural-language questions and get the correct answer from sophisticated knowledge bases built on artificial intelligence.

Traditional knowledge search tools index information with little or no customer context. As a result, the search normally results in a long list of content that must be read in hope of finding the right answer. Virtual agent software provides natural-language conversations with customers in a self-service environment or with CSRs as a knowledge-based help system. With virtual agent software, the customer or CSR types their question and gets a single answer, plus a list of the top 10 relevant FAQ's.[112] Virtual agents provide a seamless customer experience because the customer gets the same answer on the web as the CSRs do when seeking an answer on their help system.

ARE YOU PRIMING CUSTOMERS FOR RAGE OR DELIGHT?

Whether or not a customer is going to be enraged or delighted is mostly determined before they speak to your customer service resolutionary. Let me explain by walking through, what is too often, a typical customer journey.

Many studies report that half your customers try to resolve their need online before they call you. The design of your web page and mobile site, and its inability to resolve the customer's issue, has had an impact on your customer's frame of mind before they call you.

If your interactive voice response (IVR) automated phone system does not clearly, up front, enable the caller to quickly speak to a representative, then you are agitating your customer before they've even talked to a CSR. This is especially true for the half of your customers who have tried to serve themselves first online and now must go through IVR menu hell trying to find a way to talk to a representative. For this segment, we know the IVR is not going to help them if the web didn't, so why are we forcing them through the IVR menu maze?

Does your IVR require the customer to input information to identify themselves and then your representative asks the customer for the same information? If entering this information beforehand does not speed the ability of the representative to begin serving the customer, then quit asking for it in your call path menu. We know how irritating it is when young children keep asking the same question over and over. Why would we do that to our customers?

How long does it take to get a call to the agent with the right skills to resolve the issue? What tools and processes do you use to get the call routed to a qualified representative who can satisfy the customer? Any more than one transfer will only enrage your customer.

Once the customer has reached the right person, are they put on hold? Usually this is a sign of the failure of your systems and processes to empower your customer service agents with the right data before the conversation starts. Positioning for delight means having software that will push to the agent's desktop key details of who is calling, account information, and contact history before the call is answered.[113] It also means having excellent agent support tools that quickly provide answers by accessing sophisticated knowledge bases.

A customer who has tried to resolve their need online, only to resort to menu hell to get to a representative, who then asks them to repeat their account information, before transferring them, and putting them on hold is not in any mood to be delighted. They are fed up and often ready for a fight. At this point, how do you keep your CSR from appearing incompetent or rude when you've primed your customer for rage even before the conversation has started?

These examples point to the fact that leadership, by their design and resource decisions, determines whether a customer will experience rage or delight long before they get to a CSR. One of the laws of physics about call centers is that you can't fake excellence. The ability to handle millions of random calls at random times, one at a time, requires an integrated deployment of people, processes, and technology. It takes highly qualified leaders with the sufficient capital and human resources to satisfy these millions of contacts—one at a time.

It is too easy to blame CSRs for interactions that don't delight our customers when the cause is driven as much by the decisions made by executives, managers, and supervisors. The responsibility for delivering a customer who is ready for delight falls squarely on leadership's shoulders.

WHO DETERMINES AVERAGE HANDLE TIME?

In a call center, every aspect of an employee's work is measured and monitored. A typical call center representative has all their calls recorded, their screen movements tracked, the call evaluated by a supervisor, a post call customer satisfaction survey completed, their schedule adherence calculated, and the average handle time of each call computed. This wealth of performance data is not something recent because of big data. The nature of call center technology has been providing this information practically from the beginning. I've always thought that if George Orwell could walk through a call center today, he would think he was too conservative in 1949 when he wrote in his book, *1984,* about a world of big brother watching over us.

A call center is constantly challenged with balancing quality measures, such as first-contact resolution and call quality, with productivity measures, such as average handle time and schedule adherence. Unfortunately, the productivity measures often become dominant.

The *Fortune* magazine article, "Can I Help You?" captured the essence of many of today's call centers: "Call center customer service has become a finely honed discipline, but usually it seems honed to cut time: The agent is superficially friendly, but nothing can derail that person's mission of getting you off the phone fast."[114]

Interestingly, the drive to increase adoption of self-service increases average handle time (AHT) because, as stated earlier, the short, simple calls have been eliminated and you are left with the more complex, longer calls.[115] If you are holding agents to an individual AHT metric, you are putting them in double jeopardy. First, they're working against the significant headwind created by the effect of self-service adoption on AHT. Second, AHT will naturally increase as customers' present agents with the increasingly complex calls generated by a smart energy world.

AHT should not be a CSR performance metric. If your call center leadership holds individual representatives to AHT targets, then you are driving representatives to focus more on getting the customer off the phone than fulfilling their needs and building relationships. It's fine to coach those outliers who have extremely short or long AHTs. But it must be within the context of improving the customer experience and not about hitting a specific AHT target. Allowing your representatives to be customer service resolutionaries means you let the customer decide how long they want to engage.[116]

PART III

GO!

CHAPTER 14

Think Big, Smart Starts

STOP THE WORLD—I WANT TO GET OFF

Wouldn't it be great if we could stop the world so we could implement the major changes needed? The reality is, major system and process change means you must be able to overhaul the jet engines in mid-flight. Major transformations often require massive multiyear IT projects, where interim enhancements are prohibited in order to focus your limited resources on the new system replacement. As a result, years later, when the major project is complete, a long list of enhancements is needed, even though a brand-new system has just been installed. The problem is, the system you just installed was built to requirements that are now two, three, or four years old, and the world has changed. The world did not stop while you were implementing to yesterday's requirements.

How do you implement massive change that continuously meets stakeholders' requirements in a constantly changing world? I recommend a model of "Think Big, Smart Starts."

THINK BIG

Too many organizations launch projects focused on delivering specific functional capabilities without a view toward the bigger transformation required. For example, launching mobile applications without understanding how they integrate with an overall data structure and other customer service channels. Or implementing a third-party payment application without understanding how its latency in reflecting payment status fits with other existing payment applications. Implementing isolated tactical initiatives makes it unlikely you'll be able to provide a seamless customer experience across the organization.

You must "think big" so you can articulate today how you expect to serve your customers three years from now. This enables your organization to see how today's work must fit into the bigger picture in order to create the overall transformation required, rather than just a series of stand-alone tactical projects.

Constructing a think-big vision entails describing the products and services you will be delivering in three years. It also includes a description of the customer experience for each of those products and the customer interaction channels used.

SMART STARTS

It is difficult at the beginning of multiyear projects to accurately create a detailed design because things change over the years. Plus, time adds complexity to your execution. The key is that you break your think-big destination into a series of individual projects that lead to the overall transformation. I am not talking about project timeline management, but breaking the project into usable and scalable projects that deliver new functionality to the customer quickly.

For example, the United States interstate highway system was not built all at once. They thought big by having an overall vision of the routes for the entire interstate highway system. But they built it in usable sections over time and detailed the routes and the requirements as they neared the time for that section. In effect, they had a series of "smart starts" by breaking their think-big vision into small, digestible projects.

From your think-big vision, develop a series of smart starts. These are modular building block projects of defined scope and deliverables that can be released in roughly six months or less. They enable an organization to see the degree of progress and whether they are on a course to success or failure. Often "big-bang," multiyear projects don't realize they are on a path to failure until it is too late. Articulating projects that have specific deliverables with near-term delivery deadlines enables you to see whether your organization has the capabilities required to successfully implement the changes required for the think-big transformation.

Breaking transformations into defined deliverables that deliver customers new functionality quickly also provides insurance for the unpredictable future. Don't build the whole mansion over many years. Build it a room at a time, and make that room available for your customers to live in today. Then if your plans change, you at least have delivered usable functionality. Large projects can find themselves half built and not yet usable when visions, needs, resources, or passions change.

Smart starts doesn't mean a lot of pilot programs either. There are times you need pilots, but be careful. Often these are just an excuse to hedge your bet and not commit. Plus, utilities often believe they must each conduct their own pilot. As a result, the industry stays in the pilot stage and doesn't enter the transformation stage. Dynamic pricing is a good example. Jesse Berst of *Smart Grid News* says, "I've learned from experts, such as eMeter's Chris King and Brattle Group's Ahmad Faruqui, that there have already been at least 100 tests of dynamic pricing. We hardly need another." Yet we continue to hear of additional dynamic pricing pilots.[117]

If you are going to start a pilot, make sure you have clear understanding of the lessons needed. If you can't articulate the lessons needed, then you don't need a pilot. If the lessons have already been learned elsewhere, then take advantage of it. The wonderful thing about the utility industry is how willing it is to share.

A major danger in pilots is that the focus often becomes on making them work. Pilots by their nature mean you're not building real capabilities. Usually you're using the equivalent of rubber bands and duct tape to hold the pilot processes together. That is fine because that's the nature of pilots. But often the primary focus becomes making things work with limited capabilities and thus you lose sight of the lessons the pilot was to create. Anybody can make 10,000 of something work. The challenge with implementing transformations is making 1 million of something work. It is critical that your pilots maintain a focus on learning the necessary lessons for success by testing new solution models, engaging stakeholders, and determining what it will take to make things work at scale.

CHARTING THE JOURNEY TO YOUR NORTH STAR

Implementing the transformation required of customer care for our digital world means you must think big and define the overall destination. This includes defining the smart start steps of your journey, which provides clarity on what is first and what success looks like for the early phases of the journey. It also creates clarity on what the overall destination is.

Defining your North Star and charting its course involves the process, people, and technology components I discuss in the next three chapters:

- Define your desired customer care interactions: Chapter 15, "Customer Access Strategy."

- Perform an assessment of your current customer care environment: Chapter 16, "Customer Care Culture Assessment."

- Identify the high-level customer service platform capabilities, functionalities, and systems required to deliver these desired customer experiences: Chapter 17, "A New Customer Service Framework."

Customer Access Strategy

EXPONENTIAL COMPLEXITY IN CUSTOMER CARE

Utilities historically have generated a limited number of reasons for customers to contact them: among them were billing and payment, turn-on/off/transfer of service, outage reporting, and energy usage tips. As utilities engage their customers with new products and services, the number of reasons will increase to include dynamic pricing, demand response, distributed generation, prepay, gamification, and home energy services.

While utilities are adding products and services, their customers are adding numerous devices that expand their contact options. The traditional customer access channels of landline phone, cellular phone, walk-in, mail, checks, and credit cards are expanding to include smartphone, tablet, digital wallet, smart thermostat, smart watch, and countless other intelligent devices. The further expansion of consumer digital technologies will only add to the growth of customer access options.

Every new product and service, as well as each new type of customer connection, exponentially expands customer experience complexity. Customers no longer interact with you on a single channel. How they contact you varies by the device that may be the closest and most suitable to their unique need at that point in time. One time an interactive voice response (IVR) call may be great. Another time they may use their desktop PC because they are sitting in front of it. The next time it might be their smartphone app. Customers are no longer single dimensional in how they contact you, so a key think-big question is how will you align these multichannel touch points so your customer experiences across these channels meet your requirements and your customers' expectations?

WHY DO YOU DO WHAT YOU DO?

How and when your customers can access you, the level of your responsiveness, and the quality of service they receive is often a result of a series of tactical implementations rather than conscious strategic decisions. Often, your customer access parameters have been inherited through multiple generations of leadership, and no one can specify why other than "we've always done it this way." How things evolved are often the result of another department's initiatives, such as corporate communications adding a "contact us" button on the website, or adding a Facebook page, or Twitter account. What was originally a corporate communications strategy turned into a customer service channel, once it was discovered the communications channel was not being used for investor inquiries but by customers needing assistance.

I can't imagine Disney World adding a new ride or attraction without giving substantial thought to how people will interact with the new ride and how it will fit into the flow and experience of the rest of the park. So why would a business add a way for customers to contact and interact with them without considering how it impacts the total customer experience?

The reality is, if you have a branded storefront, 800 number, website, mobile app, social media page, or post office box, you have opened a customer service channel. When a customer needs something from you, they will choose the path of least resistance in search of a resolution. So it's critical you have a specific idea of what experience you want a customer to receive from each way they can access you.

MANAGE COMPLEXITY WITH A DEFINED CUSTOMER ACCESS STRATEGY

Brad Cleveland, the leading thinker on call center management, recommends a customer access strategy in order to effectively enable customers to access in real-time the resources they need. Cleveland defines a customer access strategy as "a framework—a set of standards, guidelines and processes—describing the means by which customers and the organization can interact and are enabled to access the information, services, and expertise needed."[118]

A customer access strategy forces you to consciously choose the level of quality and service you will offer through each way a customer can access your company. You must regularly review and update your customer access strategy because customers' behaviors and expectations are changing rapidly. It is important that you constantly monitor and measure your delivery in every channel against your customer access strategy.

A customer access strategy can keep you from the natural tendency to be all things to all people on all channels. Cleveland's advice: "Make your customer access strategy uniquely yours—do what's best for your customers and your organization."[119]

An effective customer access strategy includes the following components:[120]

- How customers are segmented and how the organization will serve each

- The major types of interactions that will occur for each segment

- Access channels/communities for each type of interaction

- Hours of operation for each channel

- Service level and response time objectives for each channel

- Routing methodology by customer, type of interaction, and access channel

- People/technology resources required for each segment and contact type

- Information required for the CSRs or customers

- Key information you want to capture from the contact for later analysis and improvement

- Who is responsible for maintaining the strategy and the guidelines for deploying new services

To learn more about how to create an effective customer access strategy, go to Amazon.com and order Cleveland's book, *Call Center Management on Fast Forward: Succeeding in the New Era of Customer Relationships.*

As you apply Cleveland's framework, I think you'll be surprised by the lack of clarity regarding your organization's strategy for delivering service to each customer segment. You'll readily see why a customer access strategy is critical for consistently meeting customers' expectations in an expanding multichanneled world.

CHAPTER 16

Customer Care Culture Assessment

BEST LAID PLANS...

Often plans are made and transformation initiatives started without an assessment of the culture and environment in which they will be implemented. The gravity of your existing cultural universe is powerfully strong. Most change initiatives see the light of their think-big transformation vision sucked into the black hole of their existing culture. It takes a clear understanding of your existing culture and a focused leadership effort to break free of that gravity and achieve the customer care transformation required for our digital world.

WHO ARE WE?

It is critical to understand the current customer care environment and the culture changes required to successfully implement the desired change. I recommend a series of interviews and assessments with senior leadership, managers, supervisors, and front-line service delivery employees in the following areas.

- *Clarity:* Is there a customer experience vision? Does it provide clarity to each employee as to how they should do their day-to-day job? Can employees see the role they play in the customer experience?

- *Culture*: What values and norms are detracting from or enhancing the customer experience?

- *Customer experience management:* What are the desired outcomes for key customer experiences in each major customer interaction? What desired outcomes are not being met?

- *Measures and metrics:* What measurements and metrics are in place to create clarity, align efforts, and engage employees? How effectively are performance metrics calibrated to the voice of the customer? What global-, regional-, local-, and employee-level metrics are available? Are there sufficient resources dedicated to obtaining and analyzing the transactional and perceptional metrics required? Can individual employees see their performance in the measured outcomes?

- *Employees:* How does the customer experience factor into hiring, selection, career development, and succession planning? What customer experience factors are in employee performance plans and evaluations? What incentives, rewards, and recognitions are available? What tools are available to capture the voice of the employee?

- *Governance:* What is the structure that will lead and drive the change? What is the authority of the governing counsel in relation to the existing organization and decision-making structures? How will decisions be made and resources deployed across functional organizations? What is the process for developing, monitoring, and adjusting the initiatives required in order to successfully complete the plan?

- *Alignment:* To what degree do the initiatives, culture, leadership, employees, commitment, resources, branding, timing, metrics, and rewards align with the areas requiring improvement?

WHAT DID WE LEARN?

Transforming your customer experience is not just about new technologies and improved processes. Transformations live or die with people. Organizations ingrained in a way of thinking and doing business must be moved, in lock step, with the process and technology changes required for your new desired customer experience outcomes.

Your culture assessment should provide a view of the gaps in your vision, measured outcomes, rewards, incentives, and alignment. These should be articulated into a series of initiatives in your think-big, smart starts planning.

CHAPTER 17

A New Customer Service Framework

THE MISSING SMART GRID INGREDIENT

If you're going to implement smart grid, smart meters, and smart energy, then you must change the customer experience. If you're going to interact with your customers where and how they live in this always-connected and always-on world, then you must change the customer experience. If you're going to change the customer experience, then you must think about the new systems and processes required to deliver that experience.

In all the innovation and imagining of smart energy, there has been little devoted to understanding what this smart world means for the grouping of systems the utility must deploy to support a new customer experience. Much of the thinking has been on the grid, with relatively little on how smart energy and smart customers impact your customer experience systems. Evolving your capabilities to deliver a seamless smart energy experience to your very smart customers requires a think-big strategy of how you will transform your customer service information technology taxonomy.

TIPPING THE SCALE TO A NEW IT FRAMEWORK

One of the decisions utility leaders must make is whether or not they truly are committed to changing their business model to deliver a new set of products, services, and customer experiences. The reason this is key is that it determines whether you plan to toy around with a few offerings to a few customers or are committed to delivering many new services to hundreds of thousands and millions of your customers. The reason this differentiation of true intent is key is it determines whether or not you are going to deliver at scale. As I mentioned earlier, anyone can make 10,000 of anything work. But if you are delivering something to millions it means you must be able to deliver flawlessly at scale.

Delivering smart energy to smart customers, at scale, means you must evaluate the utility's existing processes and systems to understand the change required within the utility. What changes are required in the contact center infrastructure? How are the legacy customer information systems and outage management systems impacted? How do you integrate the new systems, such as distribution management systems, demand response systems, and meter data management systems into this framework? How will you manage the increased interactions that are no longer single dimensional but conversational and multichanneled? What customer relationship, preference, and messaging management engines will you deploy? What data architecture is required to create the business intelligence capabilities to mine the big data, manage campaigns, and provide your organization the business intelligence required for a seamless customer experience?

FROM CIS TO METER-TO-ME SYSTEMS

Typically, utility customer information systems (CIS) are revenue management systems that enable utilities to manage all meter-to-cash activities. CIS is built to set a meter, bill a meter, and collect on that meter. In a smart energy world, delivering to smart customers requires a new set of capabilities to manage the customer experience. Additional customer management functionality is required to manage customer segmentation, profiles, and preferences. Increased offerings require new sales and marketing capabilities that manage product and service offerings, pricing, promotions, and campaigns. Customer account management needs the ability to go beyond the meter or premise and include individuals, families, friends, and organizations. Working with third parties to deliver new services, such as solar applications and in-home energy management systems, means you must have partner and vendor management capabilities that process contracts, provision orders, and goods, as well as generate billing and management reporting.

Telecom companies had to upgrade their legacy customer systems as their retail business became so much more than just a phone. As utilities increase their offerings of new products and services, they will need to expand their systems functionality beyond what legacy CIS systems can provide. Meter-to-cash-oriented systems will need to be upgraded with functionality that can deliver the meter-to-me services their consumers will demand.

WHEN BIG DATA WEARS THE DUNCE CAP

Utility customer service lives and dies on its CIS. These legacy systems are unique to the utility industry. Born in a world where the meter, and the premise it serves, was king. This resulted in a system built to attach data to the meter and attach the meter to a premise. This has served utilities well in a meter-to-cash world where the product is a single commodity delivered to a single meter attached to a single premise. But it is a model that will limit utilities in delivering smart energy to smart customers.

In a digital world it is about the customer. This means your data models need to be built around people, not a physical meter or premise. With your data model centered around a "party," it can represent an individual person, a group of people such as friends and family, or an organization.

The phone companies found these limitations as they went from their narrowly focused landline product to new and expanded products and services. Their premise-based data models had to change to a party model that included individual family members, each with their own set of products and services, and each with their own need for information and communication preferences. The meter or premise is no longer the center of your data model. Big data wears a dunce cap if you don't have a data model with the relationships defined in a way that is meaningful to not only your business, but more important, to your customers.

DMS IS FOR CUSTOMERS

Outage management systems (OMS) were created to help utility operators manage outage events on their systems and effectively dispatch resources to restore service to customers. Over time, these systems were then used for communicating restoration information to customers.

With the connection of digital communications to key operating components of the electrical distribution grid, distribution management systems (DMS) are being implemented to remotely manage these components to reduce the number and duration of outages.

As these new distribution operation capabilities are built, we need to keep in mind that these systems aren't just for the utilities to operate the grid better. They also are for customers. Remember, you get little credit for reliability. The customer thinks in terms of outages. The Me, Myself & I customer demands that your systems provide them information on how hard you are working for them. And when they are without power, they want to receive timely and accurate communication on the status of their restoration. When designing their smart energy taxonomy, utility operators should design their smart grid-enabled OMS and DMS as much for communicating with their customers as they do for operating the grid.

YOU'RE TOO SMALL TO BUILD IT YOURSELF

I can't imagine a CIO going in to his board and asking for millions of dollars to build his own accounting or supply-chain system? It would be a career-limiting event because who in his right mind would build a system from scratch when there are very capable, scaled, mature platforms already built and widely used?

If that's the case, why are so many utilities continuing to build their own mobile, web, and preference management capabilities? We need to understand that this new technology world is moving faster than we are. How can we hope to maintain the level of expertise required? Also, the functionality required for web, mobile, and customer management are fairly universal and, therefore, port easily to our industry. Just as accounting and supply-chain software ported to our industry years ago, so should these web, mobile, and customer engagement platforms. So why would we want to build it ourselves?

Another reason we need to quit building customer applications ourselves is because we are too small. Our industry has scale in assets but not in number of customers. You can't afford to build it yourself and spread those costs across a few million or even hundreds of thousands of customers. Customer expectations are being set by the capabilities of Starbucks, Verizon, Apple, Fidelity Investments, and on and on. All these companies are running their platforms at scale and spreading the costs across their tens of millions of customers. The largest electric utility has only 7 million customers. When you go down the list of the largest utilities, you quickly get to the majority of them being in the hundreds of thousands. It is costly to spread multimillion-dollar projects across these few customers. You need to achieve the benefits of scale by leveraging national and international platforms brought to you by solution providers.

I recently heard investment guru Jim Cramer on CNBC's *Squawk on the Street* use the term "SaaD—software-as-a-disservice." I apply his term here by using it to describe what happens when you continue to build in-house and avoid leveraging mature software-as-a-service (SaaS) alternatives. It's time to stop being SaaD.

CHAPTER 18

Universal Smart Starts

THE REALITY OF CONTEXTS

My objective in the prior chapters has been to add to your thinking of the impacts, the possibilities, and the requirements for utility customer service in our connected world. I've tried to provide thinking that is impactful in your reality and not add to the world of Pollyanna-perfect, buzzword-filled methodologies. I like to joke "all things look possible in PowerPoint." The truth is, translating bullet points into real measured success requires customer service leaders to operate within their reality.

The reality in your world is anything but perfect. Customer service leaders live in a world of organized chaos serving millions of customers, hundreds of thousands of times a day, one experience at a time. The resource, regulatory, organizational, cultural, and technology contexts are unique to each company. Your reality may be that the business case for smart meters is years away. Or the capital budget for major upgrades in your IT architecture is not available. It may be your regulators provide heavy oversight of all your customer programs, limiting your ability to innovate. Visions, goals, and initiatives all must fit into the reality of the contexts within which you must lead. You must adapt these theoretical concepts and hot trends into your own set of initiatives where they have the support, power, and resources to be successful.

Regardless of your context, there are smart starts that are universal to all organizations, which will result in think-big differences in your customers' experiences. You may not be able to go big, but the following universal smart starts can be impactful.

BUILD A BIG TABLE

It is commonplace for utilities to look to customer service as the entity that is responsible for the customer. This is natural because customer service is usually the first point of contact and many of the customer's touch points run through customer service. Yet the majority of the processes, people, and technologies delivering energy products and services lie outside of customer service. That is why customer service is "shooting pool with a rope" if they try to improve the customer experience alone. Customer care "takes a village."

From an organizational standpoint, the only true chief customer officer is the CEO. The adage "if you're not serving the customer, serve someone who does," refers to the fact that everybody is the chief customer officer. Effectively engaging customers and delivering excellent experiences requires leaders who can work across the organization and align others with the vision to make a difference in the customer's experience.

Creating a "customer council" is an effective tool for implementing change across the organization. A customer council consists of the key entities responsible for the delivery of energy and the customer experience. The council meets regularly to review customer experience performance data, identify gaps, launch initiatives, and review progress. It becomes the engine for ensuring that an excellent customer experience is consistently delivered across the organization.

A manager or supervisor may believe they are not in a position to influence and align top leadership. But regardless of your level, don't underestimate your ability to influence change. You have peers across the organization. Leverage your relationship with them in order to seize opportunities to improve customer engagement and service delivery. It is nice to have top management's commitment and support, but the reality is the real design and implementation changes occur close to the front line.

SET YOUR DASHBOARD

Employees want to do the right thing. The challenge is organizations often send mixed signals. "Satisfy the customer, follow the policy, and cut costs" don't always align. What's an employee to do?

It's critical that an organization have a "North Star" to provide general direction to what is important to the organization. Then individual departments need to create measurements that provide a clear line-of-sight to how an employee's daily activities fit into the overall picture. For example, shortly after the PSI Energy and Cincinnati Gas & Electric merger to form Cinergy, there was a need to provide clarity on the new customer experience. The following vision was provided to employees:

We make a difference in the customer's experience with Cinergy

- ...by showing respect
- ...by listening
- ...by taking ownership

- …by taking action
- …by honoring commitments

This provided clarity on the expected key employee behaviors.

After the merger of Cinergy and Duke Power, we provided customer service employees the following vision for Duke Energy:

A New Era in Customer Service.
 …New Challenges
 …New Opportunities
 …Continued Excellence

This provided clarity that although the future would bring new challenges and opportunities and many things would change, the one thing that wouldn't change was delivering excellent customer experiences.

Visions provide some clarity, but it is even more important that employees can see how their work fits into the overall vision. Build performance dashboards for each customer service group so employees can see how their work fits into the customer experience. For example, meter reading should have performance measurements of safety, number of estimated reads, and percentage of reads completed on schedule. The call center performance goals should include transactional customer satisfaction, service levels, schedule adherence, and call quality assurance scores. Success factors should be defined for each major initiative and project.

Create a clear vision and measurements of success in order to align the organization and deliver the desired customer experiences consistently across the organization.

CUSTOMER EXPERIENCE OUTCOME-BASED DESIGN

Too often great effort and resources are expended to update an offering, enhance a process, or implement a new system, only to find the mark was missed on delivering an excellent, seamless customer experience. Even with the best intentions, the results are often lacking.

Too many projects are started without a clear and specific definition of the differences to be made in the customer experience. Projects often are started with a definition outlined in terms of "implementing a new system" with a specified set of "functional requirements." I think the starting point should be defining projects in terms of specific customer experience outcomes.

A case in point was my experience in the implementation of a next-generation electronic billing and payment offering. Even though the prior electronic and billing system performed well for the majority of customers, we knew it created pain points for far too many of our customers. Usually we would have started the project by gathering a team with the objective of defining functional requirements, selecting a vendor, and implementing the new system. This time we began with a focus on learning what delighted our customers and what caused pain with our current electronic billing and payment offering. The team spent considerable hours observing, listening, and questioning employees and customers in the call centers, payment centers, and back-office processing. This led to an inventory of what delighted and pained customers, which enabled us to build a clear line of sight to the outcomes that the new offering needed to create. Following are a few examples:

Before	After
Enrollment: 24-hour wait period	Instant enrollment
A customer's existing ebill enrollment did not follow them to their new service location	A customer's existing ebill enrollment now follows them to their new service location
30-day wait period to view electronic bill	Bill can be immediately viewed upon enrollment
Did not provide real-time account balance information	Provides real-time account balance information
No email integration with email address between CRM and ebill application	Updates email information across applications

These examples may seem obvious—why would you want it any other way? The truth is that implementations quickly run into sacred cows, legacy systems, regulations, policies, procedures, and timelines that cause you to make trade-offs. It's easy to make trade-offs when success is defined more by implementing a new system by a certain date than by specific customer experience outcomes.

Do not define your project success in terms of implementing a new system and key functionalities alone. The primary success factors must be defined by specific capabilities and outcomes in the customer's terms. That way it is much harder to claim success if you're making trade-offs that sacrifice what you originally committed to deliver to your customers.

I wholeheartedly support the tools of customer journey mapping, six sigma, crowdsourcing, online portals, focus groups, and voice-of-the-customer. These data-driven learning and design tools are all very effective. My point here is that these efforts need to culminate in a very clear and specific list of customer experience outcomes that design, implementation, and success are measured against. Define success in terms of what you're delivering to your customers during those key moments of truth.

CONSISTENT EXPERIENCES ACROSS CHANNELS

Managing customer interaction was much simpler when you were limited to walk-in and phone. It got a little more complicated with the addition of the web. The addition of mobile, apps, social, and soon watches, wearables, and cars has created a new buzz phrase: "managing the multichannel customer experience."

I hear many define the omni-channel or multichannel customer experience as offering your customers numerous channels. If that is your definition, then I challenge whether the term deserves its new buzzword status. We have offered multiple channels for decades. The change is that the digital world is dramatically increasing the number of channels consumers are using. More important, these numerous digital channels have changed individual consumer behavior from consistently choosing the same channel for most of their contacts to the likelihood they will use numerous channels, depending on their situation, location, and proximity to a device. Therefore, I believe the more appropriate focus on multichannel is the provision of a consistent customer experience across all channels.

Most critical is that the data they see is the same across channels. For many industry analysts, this is a key component of omni-channel service, but doing this is usually no small effort. Often significant IT investments are required to update data architectures and customer contact systems.

Before you launch a major project to build a system of sameness across the organization, you need to understand where the biggest source of information conflict is. I think you'll find that 80 percent of the pain is in 20 percent of the data and interactions. This means you can zero in and provide relief much quicker and cheaper than you thought.

A recent utility merger created multiple customer information systems and payment alternatives, which created multiple versions of data that could be presented to customers. If new payment channel alternatives were added in the future, the situation would become even more problematic. It would be a significant investment to perfectly align the data within the legacy systems. Instead, the newly merged company created a common payment interface that enabled it to quickly and more affordably build a system that presented payment data to customers one way and then interfaced it to the numerous back-office systems. Customers could see consistent payment data and status in real-time. Then the processing and timing of each payment to its respective system was handled on the back-end, unseen to the customer.

SMALL DATA—BIG IMPACT

The utility industry is data barren compared to other industries. But that is changing rapidly as we install smart meters, distribution automation, and sensors that generate large amounts of new data. For example, it takes only 1,370 customers with smart meters capturing hourly usage data to generate the same amount of data as 1 million customers on monthly meter reading.

John von Neumann, the father of the modern computer, said, "There is no point using exact methods when there is not clarity in the concepts and issues to which they are to be applied."[121] I think von Neumann provides a useful caution as we begin the task of building competencies to pan these oceans of new data for gold. As we begin to work with utility big data, we can easily get bogged down and lose sight of what we need to know to significantly impact the business.

Fifteen years ago in our call centers, we wished we had more information on who was calling us and why. A true CRM system to capture the data was too expensive for our budget. Instead we built our "poor man's CRM" by creating an application where the customer service representative could place a checkmark on the type of call, and this data got appended to the customer account. There were errors because not all representatives were flawless in remembering to note the type of call or were consistent when interpreting the type of contact. But we began to build data that was close enough to enable us to better understand who was calling us, calling us multiple times, and why. This enabled various process improvements.

To paraphrase von Neumann, "There is no use being exact if it is not going to significantly improve the outcome." First understand what data can make the biggest difference. Then focus on the most effective way to gather the data and make a difference. It doesn't have to be perfect. It just has to be effective.

PROTECT THE LAST MOAT

Because of its importance to a utility's future, I believe outage and restoration communication is a universal smart start. While it may take a lot to move your company forward, by at least mapping where you are and where you want to be, you will have accomplished a critical universal smart start all must take.

As I mentioned earlier, technology has enabled other companies to bypass the utility and win the customer relationship. The utility's moat for energy information and control has been breached. Consumers now have many other options to choose from.

The last moat is outage and restoration information. When a customer has an outage, they cry out for information. The good news is the first place they look for information today is their utility. The even better news is the source most likely to possess this information is their utility. It is almost impossible for other organizations to provide your customers this information. However, the cry for this information is so loud that there have been instances of consumers, during major storms, building their own social network to report where they have seen crews and whether their neighborhood has been restored.

Utilities have an opportunity to make the moat wider by improving their outage restoration and communication processes as I outlined in Chapter 8 so the customer relationship with their utility for outage and restoration information is impenetrable. Ignore it, and eventually your last moat will be breached as the countless home-connected devices that today are providing video, security, and monitoring will also report outage and restoration information to a social network.

CHAPTER 19

Go Crazy!

STOP THE INSANITY

A commonly quoted definition of insanity is "doing the same thing over and over but expecting different results." Are we approaching the new customer experience challenges in the same ways we always have and expecting different results? We must recognize that the times demand new solutions and approaches.

NRG Energy CEO, David Crane, recently published a letter, in which he said:

> Occasionally I make reference to the 'Four companies that will inherit the earth,' by which I mean Amazon, Apple, Facebook, and Google. While there is a hint of facetiousness in my designation—who can predict the future in the ever-changing business world—I do have infinite respect for them, their innovativeness, the quality of the service that each provides and, most of all, the comfortable ubiquity they have achieved in the hearts and minds and everyday lives of the vast majority of people, both at home and abroad.
>
> What do these four very successful, but very distinct, companies have in common? They all provide products or services, directly to the consumer, which are deemed essential to the enrichment of their life experience, day in and day out. What

causes these four companies to rise well above others that have similar offerings? The 'Big Four' offer their own product or service in a manner that is more comprehensive, seamless, intuitive and, in the case of Apple, visually elegant, than their respective competitors. They enable, they connect, they relate, they empower.

There is no Amazon, Apple, Facebook, or Google in the American energy industry today.

There is no energy company that relates to the American energy consumer by offering a comprehensive or seamless solution to the individual's energy needs.

There is no energy company that connects the consumer with their own energy-generating potential.

There is no energy company that empowers the individual wherever they are, whatever they are doing, for however long they do it.

And there is no energy company that the consumer can partner with to combat global warming without compromising the prosperous 'plugged-in' modern lifestyle that we all aspire to—not just for us who are so blessed to live a prosperous life in the United States, but for the billions of people who live in the developing world and aspire to what we already have.[122]

Mr. Crane goes on to explain that NRG Energy is not that company either and then explains all they are doing to become that company.

I think Mr. Crane paints an effective picture of the crossroad the industry faces. A century of providing an affordable, reliable, life-changing commodity is no longer enough. Customers today demand you empower them, give them choices, and deliver seamless solutions to their individual needs.

We must stop the insanity of doing things the same way if our customers are expecting different results. We must recognize the need to change our DNA and develop new habits.

PIONEERS GET THE ARROWS; SETTLERS STAY WHERE THEY ARE

Our DNA is hard coded to be risk adverse. Seeing peers venture out of the water only to be eaten by the naysayer, just-say-no, political, self-interested prey waiting on the shore has taught us to stay put.

There's an old American West adage that says, "The pioneers get the arrows, and the settlers get the land." Implicit in this adage is that there is at least movement West. The pioneers may blaze the trail and die, but then it's the settlers who move in and form a new way of life. In our industry, the pioneers die along the trail, but no settlers move in. Having seen the pioneers die, utilities stay where they are. In effect, after numerous attempts to pioneer a new customer model, much of the industry is still sitting in St. Louis, the Gateway to the West.

We don't follow the pioneers because we are not seeing substantial rewards for the risk associated with a new life. There must be substantial rewards to not only encourage more pioneers to take risk, but to have the settlers follow and build a new way of living.

Regulators want continued control of energy prices and utility returns. Utilities want a return on their assets. Investors want a return commiserate with the risk. This three-legged stool does not support innovation and risk-taking.

BYPASS CROSSES ALL MOATS

Substantial innovation does not happen in a heavily regulated environment because it is impossible for regulators to allow substantial returns for the innovation. Would regulators ever allow an Elon Musk, Mark Zuckerberg, Larry Page, or Sergey Brin of utilities to become a multibillionaire for transforming utilities? If we expect significant energy transformation, then we need to ensure that the new energy technologies happen outside the current regulatory model.

Where would we be if mobile communications had developed under the Ma Bell model? When I was young, AT&T and their Bell Telephone monopoly owned not only the lines but also the phone in our home. Bell Labs had some of the smartest people in the world innovating amazing new communication technologies. But within this heavily regulated model, little innovation was being delivered to the customer. The focus was on a reliable, affordable, universal, homogeneous dial tone to everybody. Sound familiar?

The big consumer innovation I remember was being able to pay more for a colorful modern-looking phone in place of the black Bakelite phone. It was called the Trimline telephone. Some called it the "Princess" phone. It was first introduced in 1965. In 1966, the rotary dial was replaced with touch-tone buttons. In 1968, they added a star and a pound button to the 10 numeral buttons. In the early '70s, the clear-button back plate was replaced with an aluminum back plate, and T-jack cord connectors were introduced. In the late '70s, a power line-fed LED light replaced the incandescent lamp. In 1983, AT&T began selling phones to the public rather than their previously leased model through its newly created American Bell subsidiary. In late 1984, AT&T was divested of its regional operating companies.[123]

Take the Trimline's 20-year innovation and compare it to the last 20 years of mobile phone innovation. Is there more innovation today than in the '60s and '70s? I don't believe so. It was because the majority of wireless technologies developed outside the regulated monopolistic environment. Regulated monopolies are great at providing universal service. Competitive environments are great at innovating continual renewal. When monopolies and oligopolies can be bypassed with innovation, regardless of regulatory structures, they wither. Competitive wireless communications bypassed the landline. As a result, regardless of the regulators', monopolies', or investors' wishes, the dinosaur landline is being replaced by innovation.

The physics of electricity have limited the ability for bypass to occur. The industry is the last great monopoly whose "physics" moat still prevents the barbarians of innovation from storming the castle. Because electricity cannot be cheaply stored or made on premise, you still must connect to a large regulated monopoly distribution system. This means those who wish to innovate must still run the gauntlet of regulators and utilities that control the rules.

We need to ring fence-existing monopolies. Or at least allow the boundaries to blur as they did when the digital phone switch replaced and bypassed monopoly switchboards. New technologies that bypass utilities must be allowed to germinate outside the regulated monopoly environment. Protection of the utility model cannot be allowed at the expense of energy innovation. Major innovations require major risks. Those who take these risks must have opportunity for substantial returns. Any attempt to control solar, batteries, or demand management technologies will make the pioneers scarce and keep the settlers in St. Louis.

Our energy future requires that we all "Go West."

RETURN ON CAPITAL-LIMITING INNOVATION

The regulated-return-on-capital model has served this industry well by encouraging the building of the substantial assets required to deliver reliable energy. However, it limits the innovation required for the customer experience portions of the utility business that need to expand their capabilities but aren't capital intensive. Much of the innovations in customer service can be most effectively implemented with operations and maintenance (O&M) expenditures. However, O&M immediately comes off the bottom-line each quarter. Additionally, O&M for customer service has no capacity for earning shareholders a return. At best, you can achieve recovery of the expense in the next rate case.

Our industry's billions of dollars of prudent investments in distribution automation and advanced metering earn a regulated return. But providing the programs and services that meet the needs of the Me, Myself & I consumers comes most often from O&M dollars. This means you can only recover those dollars, not earn a return. Not allowing a return is a disincentive. In effect, spending billions on hardware, but not implementing the innovative customer-focused products and services smart grid enables, is like giving your customers an iPod but making them continue to drive to Wal-Mart to get their music.

New models must be developed that encourage utilities to use O&M expenditures for customer experiences and allows them to not only recover those expenditures, but to earn a return. We've figured out how to encourage, and allow returns on, billions of dollars in environmental, renewable, demand response, and energy efficiency expenditures. Regulators need to construct a mechanism that allows utilities to earn a return on prudent customer experience expenditures—capital and O&M.

WE NEED A BEZOS, NOT A NADER

In fairness to utilities, there are a number of stakeholders that heavily influence their customer experience model. Regulators and consumer advocates have an important role they play and often are required to advocate for a narrow customer demographic. However, the belief that utilities must provide the same level of service to all customers drives service to a much lower common denominator. I'm not minimizing the importance of their role. But who looks out for Me, Myself & I in this digital world.

The delights we are experiencing in today's customer service comes from innovators such as Amazon's Jeff Bezos or Zappos' founder Tony Hsieh. They have taken today's technologies and delivered innovations that make lives more convenient, easier, and delightful.

So who is advocating for the Me, Myself & I in our digital world? I advocate that there needs to be a "customer experience advocate" who intervenes in regulatory proceedings and advocates for the customer experience today's Me, Myself & I consumers demand.

Another approach is for regulators and utilities to construct a base level of service for all customers. Then allow utilities to provide and price other services that customers can choose from and that fall outside the traditional regulatory oversight and the regulated return and risk mitigation. For example, the Department of Energy's Green Button program, whose goal is to provide consumers easy-to-understand information regarding energy usage, encourages utilities to enable a third party, with the customer's permission, to take the meter information and provide customers with new services. These third parties are unregulated and free to offer whatever service they feel the consumer demands. And the consumer is free to choose if it is something they are willing to pay for. The consumer has a choice, and the third party is free to profit to the extent the consumer values these services. We need to allow the utility to take the same risk outside the regulated environment.

STOP THE INSANITY—GET CRAZY!

We must stop the insanity of doing things the same way and get crazy! Why crazy? Because, as originally narrated by Steve Jobs, the crazy ones change the world:

> Here's to the Crazy Ones. The misfits. The rebels. The trouble-makers. The round pegs in the square holes. The ones who see things differently. They're not fond of rules, and they have no respect for the status quo. You can quote them, disagree with them, glorify, or vilify them. About the only thing you can't do is ignore them. Because they change things. They push the human race forward. And while some may see them as the crazy ones, we see genius. Because the people who are crazy enough to think they can change the world—are the ones who do.[124]

Thank God we had Crazy Ones like Thomas Edison and Nikola Tesla. And now Elon Musk.

If you believe the smart consumer and smart energy is driving a need to transform our customer experience, where will the Crazy Ones be allowed to surface and survive within your utility? For all this technology that is descending on your organizations, the reality is that it is still people that make customers happy. Where in your organization will these Crazy Ones come from who will make the difference? Who will mentor, nurture, and support them to step outside the norm, go against the grain, and take risks? As a utility leader, you have no hope of meeting the future's requirements if you're not actively identifying, and more important, protecting the Crazy Ones.

This is a marvelous industry. It has built and operated the most complex machine in the world and improved lives beyond imagination. It is an industry I fell in love with because of the marvelous work it does and because of the people who do it. It also is an industry that frustrates me because the nature of its regulated model and its isolation from the grid, the meter, and the customer prohibits us from innovating the customer experience. Ubiquitous digital connectivity changes all of that and provides the opportunity to transform the energy experience. Your customer is already smart and getting smarter faster than you. It is time to Go Crazy!

Here's to the Crazy Ones!

Notes

1. U.S. Department of Energy, "Smart Grid."

2. U.S. Department of Energy, "Obama Administration Announces."

3. Apple Inc., video, *Apple Events*; Apple Inc., press release dated June 28, 2007, *Apple Press Info.*

4. Apple Inc., press release dated July 10, 2008, *Apple Press Info.*

5. Innovation Electricity Efficiency, *Utility-Scale Smart Meter Deployments*, 4-12.

6. Pew, "Mobile Technology Fact Sheet."

7. Apple Inc., video, *Apple Events.*

8. Ibid.

9. Bort, "Google: There Are 900 Million."

10. AppBrain, "Number of Available Android Applications."

11. Zeman, "Android's Success."

12. *Dictionary.com*, s.v. "smart."

13. Cisco, "Cisco Visual Networking Index."

14. Schadler, Bernoff, and Ask, *Mobile Mind Shift*, 46.

15. Tweed, "End of Utilities."

16. Saylor, *Mobile Wave*, 4.

17. Ibid., 2.

18. *Wikipedia*, s.v. "digital native."

19. Cleveland, *Call Center Management*, xvii.

20. Apple Inc., video, *Apple Events.*

21. AppBrain, "Number of Available Android Applications."

22. Solis, "Meet Generation C."

23. Lenhart, *Cell Phones and Amerian Adults*, 11.

24. 11mark, *IT in the Toilet.*

25. Li and Bernoff, *Groundswell*, xi–xii.

26. National Academy of Engineering, "National Academy of Engineering Reveals."

27. Heath and Seldin, *Customer Satisfaction.*

28. Bell and Patterson, *Wired and Dangerous*, 10.

29. Solomon, *High-Tech, High-Touch*, 22–25.

30. American Customer Satisfaction Index, "Scores by Industry."

31. Smith, "Customer Communications."

32. U.S. Department of Energy, Green Button.

33. Nest Labs, "Welcome to the Press Room."

34. Tilley, "Apple HomeKit."

35. J.D. Power and Associates, "Overall Customer Satisfaction."

36. Smith, "Customer Communications."

37. Conklin, "2014 Consumer Engagement Study."

38. Lowe, interview, October 20, 2014.

39. Spenner and Freeman, "To Keep Your Customers."

40. Schwartz, *Salt River Project*, 3.

41. Lowe, interview, October 20, 2014.

42. Schwartz, *Salt River Project*, 6.

43. Lowe, interview, October 20, 2014.

44. ClickFox, "Survey Findings."

45. Shaw, *Consumer Behavioral Segmentation Study*, 27.

46. St. John, "Illinois to Smart Grid."

47. OnStar, "OnStar Vehicle Diagnostics."

48. Florida Power and Light Company, "System Improvements Near You."

49. Florida Power and Light Company, "Ensuring Reliable Service."

50. Smart Grid Consumer Collaborative, "SGCC's Consumer Voices Summary."

51. King, *Willingness to Pay*, 1.

52. Ibid., 1.

53. Bing, "Cloudless Night," 190.

54. Oberle, "Senior Director, Energy Practice," 7–8.

55. Ford, *Hurricane Force "Super Derecho."*

56. iFactor, "Severe Storms."

57. Associated Press, "Utilities Better Be Ready."

58. Reuters, "Cuomo Snarls."

59. "Christie Warns NJ."

60. Carson, "Eastern Utilities."

61. Dromacque, *Innovative Smart Billing*, 8.

62. DEFG, "Prepaid Energy."

63. Lowe, interview, November 8, 2014.

64. Deloitte Center, *Deloite reSources 2014 Study*.

65. Peterson and McDermott, "Innovation in Retail Electricity Markets."

66. Rosenberg, "Oklahoma Empowers Customers."

67. Schwartz, *Salt River Project*, 2.

68. Lowe, interview, October 20, 2014.

69. J.D. Power and Associates. "Awareness and Participation."

70. Ibid.

71. Starbucks, "Starbucks 2014 Investor Day—Strategic Overview."

72. O'Dwyer, "Prepaid Energy Appeals," 2–3.

73. Krasny, "Using a Digital Wallet."

74. U.S. Department of Energy, *Voices of Experience*, 2.

75. Engagement Alliance, "What Is Gamification."

76. Anderson and Rainie, *Gamification*, 2.

77. HuffPost Live, *People Would Conserve*.

78. Lundin, "SDG&E: Changing Utility Mentality."

79. Delmarva Power, "Delmarva Challenges Customers to Save Energy for Schools."

80. *Wikipedia*, s.v. "toll-free telephone number."

81. Marsh, "40 Stats."

82. Ibid.

83. IntelliResponse, *Inside the Mind*.

84. Intelliresponse, *Mobile Self-Service*.

85. Accenture, *Actionable Insights*, 23.

86. Ragsdale, *Current State of Unassisted Support*, 12.

87. Ibid.

88. Clark, "Self-Service Trends."

89. Cantor, "Customer Effort."

90. McKendrick, *Power to the People*, 6.

91. Cisco, "Self-Service Shopping."

92. Contact Solutions, *Attitudes towards Self-Service*, 6

93. IntelliResponse, *Voice of the Customer*.

94. Bucci, *Virtual Call Agents*.

95. Martin, *Third Screen*, xxvi.

96. Ibid., xv.

97. Morris, "Mobile Matters."

98. J.D. Power and Associates, "Mobile Online Experiences."

99. Smart Grid Consumer Collaborative, *2013 State of the Consumer Report*.

100. J.D. Power and Associates, "Wide Variation."

101. Solis, *Connected Consumer*, 6.

102. Marketing Magazine, "IBM's CEO on Data."

103. Peppers and Boxer, *Leveraging Loyalty Data*.

104. Twenty First Century Communications, "Unified Customer Communications Strategy."

105. Alvarez, "Oncor Helps."

106. O'Donnell and Mikkilineni, "ComEd's Key."

107. Lowe, interview, November 8, 2014.

108. iFactor, "Georgia Power Outage Alerts."

109. Goodwin, "Best Call Center Metrics."

110. Morfas, "Knowledge Workers."

111. Minnucci, "Transform Agents."

112. IntelliResponse, *Virtual Agent vs. Site Search*.

113. Five9, "Five9 2013 Contact Center Report."

114. Colvin, "Can I Help You?," 63.

115. IntelliResponse, *Death of the Contact Center*, 2.

116. Colvin, "Can I Help You?," 63.

117. Berst, "Another Test."

118. Cleveland, *Call Center Management*, 20–21.

119. Ibid., 27.

120. Ibid., 22–25.

121. Von Neumann and Morgenstern, *Games and Economic Behavior*, quoted in Macrae, *John von Neumann*, 4.

122. Crane, "Letter from David Crane."

123. *Wikipedia*, s.v. "trimline telephone."

124. Goodreads, "Apple Inc. Quotes."

Sources

Accenture. *Actionable Insights for the New Energy Consumer.* Accessed August 17, 2012. www.accenture.com/sitecollectiondocuments/pdf/accenture-actionable-insights-new-energy-consumer.pdf.

Alvarez, Paul. "Oncor Helps Establish Best Practice on Issue Critical to Customer Satisfaction." Wired Group. May 16, 2013. http://newsletters.wiredgroup.net/?p=30.

American Customer Satisfaction Index. "Scores by Industry." Accessed October 2, 2014. www.theacsi.org/index.php?option=com_content&view=article&id=148&Itemid=213.

Anderson, Janna Quitney, and Lee Rainie. *Gamification: Experts Expect "Game Layers" to Expand in the Future, with Positive and Negative Results.* Pew Research Center. May 18, 2012. www.pewinternet.org/files/old-media/Files/Reports/2012/PIP_Future_of_Internet_2012_Gamification.pdf.

AppBrain. "Number of Available Android Applications." *AppBrain Stats.* AppTornado GmbH. Last modified September 23, 2014. www.appbrain.com/stats/number-of-android-apps.

Apple Inc. Press release. *Apple Press Info.* June 28, 2007. www.apple.com/pr/library/2007/06/28iPhone-Premieres-This-Friday-Night-at-Apple-Retail-Stores.html.

———. Press release. *Apple Press Info.* July 10, 2008. www.apple.com/pr/library/2008/07/10iPhone-3G-on-Sale-Tomorrow.html.

———. Video of 2014 Worldwide Developers Conference. *Apple Events.* June 2, 2014. www.apple.com/apple-events/june-2014/.

Associated Press. "Patrick: Utilities Better Be Ready for Storm." *Boston Globe*, October 25, 2012. www.boston.com/news/weather/2012/10/25/partrick-utilities-better-be-ready-for-storm/LW2XlhQm4ji8qtHU2on0N/story.html.

Bell, Chip R., and John R. Patterson. *Wired and Dangerous: How Your Customers Have Changed and What to Do about It.* San Francisco: Berrett-Koehler, 2011.

Berst, Jesse. "Sigh, Yet Another Test of Dynamic Pricing: Will We Believe It This Time?" *SmartGridNews.* March 20, 2013. www.smartgridnews.com/story/sigh-yet-another-test-of-dynamic-pricing-will-we-believe-it-time/2013-03-19?fpt.

Bing, Stanley. "A Cloudless Night." *Fortune*, July 23, 2012.

Bort, Julie. "Google: There Are 900 Million Android Devices Activated." *Business Insider*, May 5, 2013. www.businessinsider.com/900-million-android-devices-in-2013-2013-5.

Bucci, Dick. *Mastering Self-Service with Virtual Call Agents.* VPI. Accessed September 13, 2013. www.vpi-corp.com/Virtual-Agent-Paper/.

Cantor, Brian. "Why Customer Effort Is the Right Approach for Customer Service." Customer Management IQ. August 8, 2013. www.customermanagementiq.com/cem-value-added-customer-adoption-path/articles/why-customer-effort-is-the-right-approach-for-cust/.

Carson, Phil. "Eastern Utilities and Another Hard Lesson." July 2, 2012. Energy Central. www.intelligentutility.com/article/12/07/eastern-utilities-and-another-hard-lesson.

"Christie Warns NJ about Hurricane Chris." *Courier-Post*, November 7, 2012. www.courierpostonline.com/ar.../Christie-warns-NJ-utilities-about-Hurricane-Chris-?odyssey=nav|.

Cisco Systems, Inc. "Cisco Visual Networking Index: Global Mobile Data Traffic Forecast Update, 2013–2018." February 5, 2014. www.cisco.com/c/en/us/solutions/collateral/service-provider/visual-networking-index-vni/white_paper_c11-520862.html.

———. "Self-Service Shopping Grows in Popularity, according to Cisco Study." June 5, 2013. newsroom.cisco.com/press-release-content?type=webcontent&articleid=1200551.

Clark, Cynthia. "Self-Service Trends: Helping Customers Serve Themselves." 1to1 Media. March 4, 2013. www.1to1media.com/View.aspx?docid=34129.

Cleveland, Brad. *Call Center Management on Fast Forward: Succeeding in the New Era of Customer Relationships.* Colorado Springs, CO: ICMI, 2012.

ClickFox. "Survey Findings: Mobile Apps for Customer Service."
August 7, 2012. web.clickfox.com/2011SurveyResults-Mobile-
AppsforCustomerService.html.

Colvin, Geoffrey. "Can I Help You?" *Fortune*, April 30, 2012.

Conklin, Jeff. "2014 Consumer Engagement Study: Overview
Webcast Results." J. D. Power and Associates. May 22, 2014.
www.jdpower.com/sites/default/files/2014%20Utility%20Pro-
gram%20Engagement%20Webcast%20PPT%20Deck%20
FINAL%205.22.14.pdf

Contact Solutions. *2013 Consumer Attitudes towards Self-Service.*
August 2013. contactsolutions.sits.hubspot.com/consumer-
attitudes-towards-self-service-2013-survey?

Crane, David. "Letter from David Crane, CEO of NRG." NRG.
March 26, 2014. www.nrgenergy.com/ceoletter/.

DEFG. "Prepaid Energy Leads to 11% Drop in Energy Consumption, Report Finds." March 22, 2013. http://defgllc.com/news/
article/prepaid-energy-leads-to-11-drop-in-energy-consump-
tion-report-finds/.

Delmarva Power. November 8, 2012. www.delmarva.com/library/
templates/Interior.aspx?Pageid=847&id=15262.

Deloitte Center for Energy Solutions. *Deloite reSources 2014
Study*. Accessed December 6, 2014. www2.deloitte.com/
content/dam/Deloitte/us/Documents/energy-resources/us-er-
resources%202014-study.pdf.

Dictionary.com, s.v. "smart." Accessed August 15, 2014. http://dic-
tionary.reference.com/.

Dromacque, Christophe. *Case Study on Innovative Smart Billing for
Household Consumers.* World Energy Council Case Studies.
July 15, 2013. www.wec-policies.enerdata.eu/Documents/
cases-studies/Smart_Billing.pdf.

11mark. *IT in the Toilet.* January 30, 2012. www.11mark.com/IT-
in-the-Toilet.

Engagement Alliance. "What Is Gamification.[*sic*]" December 5,
2014. engagementalliance.org/what-is-gamification/.

Five9. "Five9 2013 Contact Center Report: Calming Customer
Rage in the Modern Service Era." November 14, 2013. www.
five9.com/customer-experience-report.

Florida Power and Light Company. "Ensuring Reliable Service."
Accessed August 12, 2012. www.fpl.com/residential/power_
quality/powerful_solutions.shtml.

————. "System Improvements Near You." Accessed August 12, 2012. http://www.fplmaps.com/map/map.shtml.

Ford, Michelle. *Hurricane Force "Super Derecho" Hits Midwest & Atlantic States.* Twenty First Century Communications Inc. August 16, 2012. blog.tfcci.com/.

Goodreads. "Apple Inc. Quotes." http://www.goodreads.com/quotes/924-here-s-to-the-crazy-ones-the-misfits-the-rebels-the.

Goodwin, Rich. "What Are the Best Call Center Metrics for a Great Customer Experience?" *E Source Blog,* June 5, 2012. www.esource.com/Blog/ESource/6-5-12-CallCenterMetrics.

Heath, Andrew, and Dan Seldin. *How Customer Satisfaction Drives Return on Equity for Regulated Electric Utilities: A J.D. Power and Associates White Paper.* J. D. Power and Associates. May 2012. www.jdpower.com/content/white-paper/OR5NSWv/how-customer-satisfaction-drives-return-on-equity-for-regulated-utilities.htm.

HuffPost Live. *People Would Conserve Energy If It Were A Game!* (video report). August 21, 2012. live.huffingtonpost.com/t/segment/people-would-conserve/502e77cf02a7605f1a00057b.

iFactor. "Georgia Power Outage Alerts Add Value for Customers." December 17, 2013. www.ifactorconsulting.com/georgia-power-outage-alerts-add-value-for-customers-website-tools-make-registration-easy/.

————. "iFactor Consulting: Severe Storms Create High Demand for Communication." August 23, 2012. www.ifactorconsulting.com/severe-storms-create-high-demand-for-communication/.

Innovation Electricity Efficiency. *Utility-Scale Smart Meter Deployments: A Foundation for Expanded Grid Benefits.* August 2013. www.edisonfoundation.net/iee/Documents/IEE_SmartMeterUpdate_0813.pdf.

IntelliResponse. *Death of the Contact Center.* April 23, 2013. info.intelliresponse.com/rs/intelliresponse/Images/Death%20of%20the%20Call%20Center.pdf.

————. *Inside the Mind of Your Customers.* August 8, 2014. www.intelliresponse.com.

————. *Mobile Self-Service: The New Lynchpin of Customer Engagement.* October 11, 2012. info.intelliresponse.com/rs/intelliresponse/images/Mobile_Self_Service_WP.pdf.

————. *Virtual Agent vs. Site Search.* Accessed April 21, 2013. info. intelliresponse.com/WhitePapers_VAvsSiteSearch.html.

————. *Voice of the Customer: The New Digital Frontier.* 2013. info. intelliresponse.com/WhitePapers_VOC_2013.html.

J.D. Power and Associates. "Awareness and Participation in Electric Utility Offerings Increases Overall Satisfaction." July 23, 2013. www.jdpower.com/content/press-release/sCbperj/2013-consumer-engagement-study.htm.

————. "Mobile Online Experiences at Utility Websites Failing to Meet Customers' Expectations." April 10, 2013. www.jdpower.com/content/press-release/qigF42u/2013-utility-website-evaluation-study.htm.

————. "Overall Customer Satisfaction with Residential Electric Utilities Continues to Improve; However, Utilities Not Keeping Pace with Satisfaction Increases in Other Service Industries." J.D. Power Press Releases. July 16, 2014. www.jdpower.com/press-releases/2014-electric-utility-residential-customer-satisfaction-study.

————. "Wide Variation in Consumer Knowledge and Behaviors Poses Daunting Challenge to Building Engagement with Smart Energy Technologies." October 24, 2011. http://businesscenter.jdpower.com/news/pressrelease.aspx?ID=2011178.

King, Kathleen. *Willingness to Pay to Avoid Outages: Reliability Demand Survey.* Washington, DC: Bates White Economic Consulting, 2012.

Krasny, Jill. "Everyone and Their Mother Will Soon Be Using a Digital Wallet." May 10, 2012. www.businessinsider.com/everyone-and-their-mother-will-soon-be using-a-digital-wallet-2012-5.

Lenhart, Amanda. *Cell Phones and American Adults.* Pew Research Center. September 2, 2010. www.pewinternet.org/2010/09/02/cell-phones-and-american-adults/.

Li, Charlene, and Josh Bernoff. *Groundswell: Winning in a World Transformed by Social Technologies.* Boston: Forrester Research, 2011.

Lowe, Mike. Interview by Todd W. Arnold. October 20, 2014.

————. Interview by Todd W. Arnold. November 8, 2014.

Lundin, Barbara Vergetis. "SDG&E: Changing Utility Mentality." April 8, 2013. www.fierceenergy.com/story/sdge-changing-utility-mentality/2013-04-08.

Marketing Magazine. "IBM's CEO on Data, the Death of Segmenta-
    tion and the 18-Month Deadline." February 13, 2013.
    www.marketingmag.com.au/news/ibms-ceo-on-data-the-death-
    of-segmentation-and-the-18-month-deadline-36359/#.VJVz-
    pAJA.

Marsh, Amanda. "40 Stats Shaping the Future of Contact Centers."
    VPI blog. March 5, 2013. http://blog.vpi-corp.com/blog/
    performance-optimization-2/40-stats-shaping-the-future-of-
    contact-centers.

Martin, Chuck. *The Third Screen.* Boston: Nicholas Brealey, 2011.

McKendrick, Joseph. *Power to the People: Online Self-Service Evolves.*
    New Providence, NJ: Unispher Research, 2013.

Minnucci, Jay. "Transform Agents from Transaction Processors
    to Knowledge Workers." Pipeline Online. November 13,
    2012. www.contactcenterpipeline.com/PipelineOnline/
    po20121113_Static.htm.

Morfas, Dave. "Knowledge Workers: Modern Day 'Resolution-
    aries.'" Accessed November 2, 2012. www.aptean.com/uk/
    assets/pdfs/resources/documents/APT-WP-KnowWorkersMo-
    dernDayRes.pdf.

Morris, Tricia. "Mobile Matters: 10 Must-Read Mobile Customer
    Engagement Statistics." October 2, 2013. www.parature.com/
    mobile-matters/.

National Academy of Engineering. "National Academy of Engineer-
    ing Reveals Top Engineering Impacts of the 20th Century:
    Electrification Cited as Most Important." National Academy
    of Engineering. February 22, 2000. www.nationalacademies.
    org/greatachievements/Feb22Release.PDF.

Nest Labs. "Welcome to the Press Room." May 7, 2013. nest.com/
    press/nest-acquires-myenergy/.

Oberle, Chris. "Senior Director, Energy Practice." In *Chartwell 2011
    Outage Communications Summit* (hard copy of PowerPoint pre-
    sentation; used with permission). San Diego: Chartwell, 2011.

O'Donnell, Gene, and Mahesh Mikkilineni. "ComEd's Key to
    Effective Utility Customer Communications in an Outage."
    October 17, 2013. www.greentechmedia.com/articles/read/
    ComEds-Key-to-Effective-Utility-Customer-Communica-
    tions-in-an-Outage.

O'Dwyer, Cindy Boland. "Prepaid Energy Appeals to Consumers
    in a Connected World." Distributed Energy Financial Group

LLC / EcoAlign. 2013. defgllc.com/publication/prepaid-
energy-appeals-to-consumers-in-a-connected-world/.

OnStar. "OnStar Vehicle Diagnostics." Email to the author from
OnStar Subscriber Services,

Peppers, Don, and Melissa Boxer. *Leveraging Loyalty Data to
Enhance the Cross-Channel Customer Experience.* 1to1 Executive
Dialogue. Accessed November 2, 2012. www.1to1media.com/
Thankyou.aspx?Docid=33592.

Peterson, Carl R., and Karl A. McDermott. "Innovation in Retail
Electricity Markets: The Overlooked Benefit." Compete Coali-
tion. March 2008. www.competecoalition.com/resources/
innovation-retail-electricity-markets-overlooked-benefit.

Pew Research Center's Internet & American Life Project. "Mobile
Technology Fact Sheet." Pew Research Center. Last modified
January 2014. http://pewinternet.org/facts-sheets/mobile-
technology-fact-sheet/.

Ragsdale, John. *The Current State of Unassisted Support.* San Diego:
TSIA Research, 2011.

Reuters. "Cuomo Snarls at Power Companies as Lights Stay Out."
CNBC U.S. Business News. November 2, 2012. www.cnbc.
com/id/49623985 (article no longer available online).

Rosenberg, Martin. "Oklahoma Empowers Customers—Big Time."
March 3, 2013. www.energybiz.com/article/13/02/oklahoma-
empowers-customers-big-time-1.

Saylor, Michael. *The Mobile Wave.* New York: Vanguard Press, 2012.

Schadler, Ted, Josh Bernoff, and Julie Ask. *The Mobile Mind Shift.*
Cambridge, MA: Groundswell Press, 2014.

Schwartz, Judith. *Salt River Project (SRP): The Persistence of Con-
sumer Choice.* Association for Demand Response & Smart
Grid. June 15, 2012. www.demandresponsesmartgrid.org/
Resources/Documents/Case%20Studies/SRP_CaseStudy_
Final_061812.pdf.

Shaw, Peter, et al. *2011 Smart Energy Consumer Behavioral Segmentation Study.* Westlake Village, CA: J.D. Power and Associates,
2011.

Smart Grid Consumer Collaborative. "SGCC's Consumer Voices
Summary." May 2012. smartgridcc.org/research/sgcc-research/
sgccs-consumer-voices-summary.

———. *2013 State of the Consumer Report.* January 21, 2013.
smartgridcc.org/sgccs-2013-state-of-the-consumer-report.

Smith, Dennis. "Customer Communications Is an Integral Part of the Outage Restoration Process." *Energy Blog*, July 20, 2012. J.D. Power and Associates. www.jdpowercontent.com/energyblog/customer-communications-is-an-integral-part-of-the-outage-restoration-process/2012/07/20/.

Solis, Brian. *The Connected Consumer and the New Decision-Making Cycle*. IBM. September 24, 2013. www-01.ibm.com/common/ssi/cgi-bin/ssialias?infotype=SA&subtype=ST&htmlfid=ZZU12352USEN#loaded.

———. "Meet Generation C: The Connected Customer." April 9, 2012. www.briansolis.com/2012/04/meet-generation-c-the-connected-customer/.

Solomon, Micah. *High-Tech, High-Touch, Customer Service*. New York: AMACOM, 2012.

Spenner, Patrick, and Karen Freeman. "To Keep Your Customers, Keep It Simple." *Harvard Business Review*, May 2012. Reprinted by The Corporate Executive Board (CEB) at www.executiveboard.com/exbd/marketing-communications/decision-simplicity/index.page.

St. John, Jeff. "Illinois to Smart Grid: Prove You're Worth It—or Pay." Greentech Media. December 9, 2011. www.greentechmedia.com/articles/read/illinois-to-smart-grid-prove-youre-worth-it-or-pay.

Starbucks. "Starbucks 2014 Investor Day—Strategic Overview." Report presented at Starbucks 2014 Biennial Investor Day, December 4, 2014. investor.starbucks.com/phoenix.zhtml?c=99518&p=irol-presentations.

Tilley, Aaron. "How Apple HomeKit Is Already Changing the Smart Home Industry." *Forbes*, September 8, 2014. www.forbes.com/sites/aarontilley/2014/09/08/why-this-smart-device-maker-chose-apple-over-google-in-the-smart-home/.

Tweed, Katherine. "The End of Utilities." Greentech Media. April 29, 2011. www.greentechmedia.com/articles/read/the-end-of-utilities/.

Twenty First Century Communications. "Unified Customer Communications Strategy." (PowerPoint presentation; used with permission). March 8, 2013.

U.S. Department of Energy. Green Button. Accessed September 24, 2014. energy.gov/data/green-button.

————. "Smart Grid." Accessed June 22, 2012. http://energy.gov/oe/technology-development/smart-grid.

————. "Obama Administration Announces Availability of $3.9 Billion to Invest in Smart Grid Technologies and Electric Transmission Infrastructure." June 25, 2009. http://energy.gov/articles/obama-administration-announces-availability-39-billion-invest-smart-grid-technologies-and.

————. *Voices of Experience: Insights on Smart Grid Customer Engagement.* SmartGrid.gov. December 20, 2014. www.smartgrid.gov/sites/default/files/VoicesofExperience_Brochure_9.26.2013.pdf.

Von Neumann, John, and Oskar Morgenstern. *Theory of Games and Economic Behavior.* 60th anniversary ed. Princeton, NJ: Princeton University Press, 2004. First published 1944.

Wikipedia, s.v. "digital native." Accessed February 28, 2013. http://en.wikipedia.org/.

Wikipedia, s.v. "toll-free telephone number." Accessed February 19, 2013. http://en.wikipedia.org/wiki/toll-free_telephone_number.

Wikipedia, s.v. "trimline telephone." Accessed April 3, 2014. http://en.wikipedia.org/wiki/Trimline_telephone.

Zeman, Eric. "Android's Success: By the Numbers." *Information Week*, February 28, 2012. www.informationweek.com/news/mobility/smart_phones/232601613.

Index

P

pain points, 43, 135
Patrick, Deval, 55
payment fees, 69–70
payment options, 68–71
performance measures, 49, 107, 122, 134
Persistence of Consumer Choice, The (Schwartz), 44
Peterson, Carl R., 66–67
Pew Internet research, 5, 19
pilot programs, 113–114
pioneers, 148
planned outages, 51
Power to the People: Online Self-Service Evolves study, 83
Prensky, Marc, 14
prepaid electricity, 69
presentment level of customer engagement, 35, 37
PSI Energy, 133
public relations, 52
pushback from customers, xviii, 31

R

rate options, 66
reality of contexts, xxiv, 131–132
reconnect fees, 72
relationships, need for, 29–31. *See also* customer engagement
reliability
    apps for reporting on, 94
    companies that are rethinking, 50–51
    expectation of, 60
    rethinking, 51–52
    of U.S. electricity, 47–48
requirements for customer service/engagement
    doing something for Me, Myself & I customers, 41–43
    making it easy, 44–45
    making the delivery flawless, 45–46

resolution of problems. *See also* self-service; trusted energy resolutionaries (CSRs)
    average handle time, 106–107
    fingertip interactions, 89–92, 93–94
    first-contact, 84
    rates of self-service, 83
responsiveness, level of, 118–119
restoration information, 55–56, 56–60, 139–140
return on equity (ROE), 29
return on investments (ROI), 36
risk-taking, 143, 148
ROE (return on equity), 29
ROI (return on investments), 36
Rometty, Ginni, 97

S

SaaD (software-as-a-disservice), 130
SaaS (software-as-a-service), 130
SAIDI (System Average Interruption Duration Index), 49
SAIFI (System Average Interruption Frequency Index), 49
Salt River Project (SRP), 43, 64, 67–68, 100
San Diego Gas & Electric (SDG&E), 74–75
satisfaction of customers, 67–68, 133
Saylor, Michael, 9–10
Schadler, Ted, 8
Schwartz, Judith, 44
SDG&E (San Diego Gas & Electric), 74–75
search tools, 103
segmentation, 95–96
self-service, 45–46
    average handle time increases through, 106–107
    benefits of offering, 102
    changing to MySelf Service, 80–82 (*See also* MySelf Service)
    Cisco study, 85–86

CPSIA information can be obtained
at www.ICGtesting.com
Printed in the USA
LVOW03*1927100418
572977LV00002B/9/P

9 780996 136006